Mozart

Mozart at the piano (unfinished oil painting by Joseph Lange, 1782)

STANLEY SADIE

Mozart

Illustrated Calderbook CB.71

CALDER AND BOYARS · LONDON

This edition first published in Great Britain 1965
by Calder and Boyars Ltd
18 Brewer Street London W1

Second edition 1970

SBN 7145 0067 4 Cloth edition
SBN 7145 0068 2 Paper edition

PRINTED IN GREAT BRITAIN BY
FLETCHER AND SON LTD NORWICH

Mozart
by Stanley Sadie

Contents

Leopold Mozart and his two children (watercolour by Carmontelle, 1763)

The Infant Prodigy

The course of musical history is marked by periods of revolution and periods of evolution. In the decade of Mozart's birth, the 1750s, a minor revolution had just taken place. The contrapuntal grandeur of the musical language of the baroque era, seen at its greatest in Bach and Handel, had been displaced by a new idiom based on simpler ideals of melody and expressiveness. Mozart was to work during a period of evolution— of consolidation, extension and deepening—and was to die before the next stage of revolution came.

Mozart was born, on the 27th of January 1756, into a musical home. His father, Leopold Mozart, who came from a bookbinders' family at Augsburg, had settled in Salzburg after studying at the university there. He had married a local woman, Maria Anna Pertl, and was a violinist in the orchestra at the Archbishop of Salzburg's court. (The prince-archbishops of Salzburg, who play an important part in the story of Mozart's life, were in reality more temporal than spiritual lords.) Leopold Mozart was a competent composer who wrote a good deal of music, mostly of an indifferent and routine quality. But as a performer and teacher of the violin he was extremely able. In 1756 he published a tutor for the instrument, which achieved considerable fame and was translated into several languages; it still remains invaluable to the student interested in the authentic performance of old music.

Joannes Chrysostomus Wolfgangus Theophilus, to give him his full baptismal names, was one of two survivors of the seven children born to Leopold and his wife. The other was Maria Anna, or Nannerl, his elder by four-and-a-half years. When only two or three Wolfgang, hearing her harpsichord lessons, began to show a keen interest in music. There are countless tales of his quite extraordinary musical gifts as a child. At three he was picking out euphonious chords on the harpsichord; at four he was playing short pieces; at five he was composing—some of these brief early efforts are preserved, in his father's handwriting. He even attempted to write a harpsichord concerto at this early age. Not many years later, he amused his father and a friend by asserting that the friend's violin was tuned an eighth of a tone lower than his own: but amusement turned to wonder when the boy was demonstrated to be correct. His progress on the violin was as phenomenal as in every other musical sphere. Once he astonished his father and two other musicians by taking over the second violin part in some trios, playing it at sight in exemplary fashion.

But above all it was his harpsichord playing which excelled, and Leopold not unnaturally felt that this divine gift could be exploited jointly to the glory of God and the profit of the Mozart family. So about the time of Wolfgang's sixth birthday he and his almost equally talented sister were whisked off to Munich to appear before the Elector of Bavaria. Father and children returned after some three weeks, amply recompensed for their trouble and probably laden with the useless gifts which it was customary for noblemen to dispense on such occasions.

In September of the same year Leopold obtained leave of absence from the easy-going Archbishop for another, more ambitious jaunt, to Vienna. On the way the family stopped at Passau to play to the Bishop and at Linz to give a concert. Rumours of the children's abilities had reached the imperial capital before their arrival. Soon they were commanded to appear at Schönbrunn, where they much impressed the Emperor and Empress: the children were sent gifts of elaborate court clothes discarded by growing members of the royal family and Leopold was given money. Their time in the capital was largely spent visiting noble music-lovers anxious to enthuse over the wonder-children. At one concert where Wolfgang was to play a concerto by Wagenseil, a leading figure in Vienna's musical life, he perhaps rather undiplomatically asked that the composer should come to turn the pages for him. An attack of scarlet fever interrupted the triumphal progress, but not for long, and the trip ended with a visit to Pressburg at the request of a group of Hungarian noblemen.

One might well wonder what effect all this fêting had on a sensitive child. No doubt he was already beginning to develop a realistic—that is, an exceedingly high—estimation of his own capabilities. Some of his behaviour certainly suggests spoiled, not merely uninhibited, behaviour: for example, his leaping on to the Empress' lap and kissing her, or his offer of marriage to Princess Marie Antoinette when she picked him up after a tumble, and his disdain of her less kindly sister. Although he had a normal childish sense of humour he was not exactly a normal child. Arithmetic and his other studies interested him, but music was his sole devotion and he took it desperately seriously. He was unusually emotional and affectionate, especially towards his father.

They had been home a mere four months when Leopold decided it was time to be off once more, not simply for a few weeks at a nearby city but for a grand tour of Europe lasting more than three years. In June 1763 the whole family set out. The first main city to visit was Munich, where the children played to the Elector; after ten days they moved on to Augsburg, visiting Leopold's brothers and, since the town had no court, giving three public concerts. Neither stop proved very profitable, to Leopold's chagrin (expressed in letters to his friend and landlord at Salzburg, Lorenz Hagenauer). Ludwigsburg, summer residence of the Duke of Wurtemburg's court, was their next call. There the illustrious Niccolò Jommelli was head of the musical establishment, which was largely Italian and included the famous violinist Nardini. Jommelli marvelled that a German child could perform such feats but, according to the mistrustful Leopold, ensured that the Duke—who in any case was ungenerous to visitors—had no opportunity to share his wonder.

Entrance to the house of Mozart's birth, now a Mozart Museum

The next stop was Schwetzingen, summer residence of the Palatine court. Here they heard the magnificent Mannheim orchestra, which under its original director, Johann Stamitz, had helped to create the prevailing style of orchestral music. At the sophisticated, Frenchified court, the Elector and Electress were delighted by the children's playing. Then after a visit to Heidelberg, where Wolfgang astonished everyone by his brilliance on the church organ, on to Mainz: there could be no concert at court as the Elector was ill, but three public ones compensated.

At Frankfurt their concert was so successful that it had to be given four times over—Goethe, then a boy of fourteen, was among the enthusiastic audience. We know from an advertisement what sort of performance the children offered. Both of them played the harpsichord, then Wolfgang played a violin concerto and the harpsichord continuo parts in symphonies (with a cloth covering his hands); he named notes played singly or in chords, and improvised on the harpsichord and organ. From Frankfurt they went to Coblenz, playing at court; then, stopping at Bonn and Cologne as tourists rather than musicians, to Aachen, where Princess Amalia of Prussia was generous with her kisses for the children —which, Leopold ruefully reflected, would not pay innkeepers' bills or travelling expenses.

Now the family left German territory and entered the Austrian Netherlands (present-day Belgium). Travelling through Liège and Louvain, they arrived in Brussels at the beginning of October. Here they were kept awaiting the pleasure of Prince Charles of Lorraine; they could neither give a concert nor leave the city without his permission. Generous gifts were showered on them by the courtiers at whose houses they played—Leopold joked about opening a stall for snuff-boxes and suchlike trinkets. Eventually they gave a very successful public concert, attended by the Prince.

In mid-November they left for Paris, one of the great musical centres. Here they stayed in the house of the Bavarian Ambassador, and were soon befriended by Grimm, a German who had lived in the city for many years and was prominent in artistic and intellectual circles. Most of their letters of introduction were ignored, and it was probably Grimm who arranged for them to go to Versailles to perform at court. At a New Year's Day banquet the family were allowed to watch, Wolfgang standing by the Queen, talking to her and tasting morsels from the table. After this they were invited to the houses of many leading families and even managed to obtain permission to give two semi-public concerts. While in Paris they met some of the leading composers there, such as Schobert, Eckard and Honauer—all Germans, for Leopold, like every non-Frenchman, heartily despised the native product. During his stay Wolfgang wrote and published a set of four sonatas for keyboard with violin accompaniment. It was the first of his music to appear in print.

After Paris, only London would do. They saw the sea for the first time in their lives, and felt its effects too on the crossing from Calais to

Leopold Mozart (oil painting, probably by Lorenzoni, c.1765)

Dover. Within five days of their arrival in the capital on the 22nd of April 1764 they appeared at court, being delighted by the charm and informality of their welcome from George III and his German-born consort—as well as by the promptness of their twenty-four guinea reward. The London season was over, but a concert early in June, when the city was full on account of the King's birthday, helped to make them known and earned them a hundred guineas. Wolfgang also appeared at a benefit concert for a new lying-in hospital, 'one way of winning the affection of this quite exceptional nation',★ Leopold wrote. Their plans received a setback when Leopold fell ill. It was nothing serious, but he was a chronically anxious man and looked after himself with the greatest assiduity, even moving to the riverside village of Chelsea for the better air.

While he was ill, silence from the children was essential. So the nine-year-old Wolfgang busied himself with composition. At this time he wrote his first two symphonies and a further set of accompanied sonatas, which were published in London and dedicated to the Queen. Another work written in England was the 'madrigal' *God is our refuge*, presented by Wolfgang to the British Museum, where it has been ever since.

London's leading musical figure was John Christian Bach, J. S. Bach's youngest son, who had settled in the city in 1762. He was a kindly, benevolent man and immediately took to the gifted child. An English musician, William Jackson, heard them playing together and left an account of the occasion which is little known:

'When [Mozart] was a mere infant . . . he was exhibited as a great performer on the harpsichord, and an extraordinary genius for music. John Bach took the child between his knees and began a subject on the

★Quotations from the letters of Mozart and his family are taken, by kind permission, from the English versions by Emily Anderson.

A view of the Thames (after Canaletto)

The house in Ebury Street, London, where the Mozart family lodged

instrument, which he left, and Mozart continued— each led the other into very abstruse harmonies, and extraneous modulations, in which the child beat the man. We were afterwards looking over Bach's famous song "Se spiego" in *Zanaïda*. The score was inverted to Mozart, who was rolling on the table. He pointed out a note which he said was wrong. It was so, whether of the composer or copyist I cannot now recollect, but it was an instance of extraordinary discernment and readiness in a mere infant.'

For the Benefit of Mifs MOZART of Thirteen, and Mafter MOZART of Eight Years of Age, Prodigies of Nature.
HICKFORD's Great Room in Brewer Street, This Day, May 13. will be A CONCERT of VOCAL and INSTRUMENTAL MUSIC. With all the OVERTURES of this little Boy's own Compofition.
The Vocal Part by Sig. Cremonini; Concerto on the Violin Mr. Bartholemon; Solo on the Violoncello, Sig. Cirii; Concerto on the Harpfichord by the little Compofer and his Sifter, each fingle and both together, &c.
Tickets at 5 s. each, to be had of Mr. Mozart, at Mr. Williamfon's, in Thrift-ftreet, Soho.
For the Benefit of Mr. KEEN and Mr.

From 'The Public Advertiser', 13th May, 1765

The Mozarts spent more than a year and a quarter in London. Leopold's frank avarice at the thought of the hundreds of guineas to be pocketed made him in no hurry to leave. They again appeared at court and gave more public concerts, with Wolfgang's new symphonies in the programmes. Towards the end of their stay, Leopold threw open their Soho lodgings at certain hours to anyone who cared to satisfy himself of the children's genius by closer examination; and with a characteristically English enquiring spirit, the philosopher Daines Barrington subjected Wolfgang to a really searching test, the results of which he later published. The musical historian Charles Burney also wrote a learned paper about the prodigious infant. A proposal was made to Leopold about settling in England, but after much heart-searching he rejected it because of the dangerous and irreligious environment for bringing up children.

At the end of July they finally bade farewell to London, breaking their journey to Dover at Canterbury to stay with friends and see some horse racing. There a message reached them from the Princess of Weilburg, sister of the Prince of Orange, who was very anxious to see and hear the children. Her interesting condition made it impossible to refuse, so plans for the homeward journey had to be modified to take in a tour of the Dutch musical centres. More modifications had to be made at Lille, where first Wolfgang had a bad cold and then Leopold was ill again. After a month's delay they moved on through Ghent, Antwerp and Rotterdam to The Hague. Leopold was much taken with the cleanliness of the Dutch towns, also commenting on the many fine pictures to be

Nannerl Mozart (oil painting, probably by Lorenzoni, 1763)

seen and the excellent organs, some of which Wolfgang tried. In The Hague they appeared at court and gave a public concert.

Now it was Nannerl's turn to be ill—so ill, indeed, that extreme unction was administered. Just as she was recovering Wolfgang succumbed again, and in four weeks was reduced to skin and bone. But by January 1766 he was fit enough to spend a few weeks in Amsterdam and appear in two concerts, at one of which his newest symphony was played. Then back to The Hague, with another performance at court on the occasion of the Prince's coming-of-age, for which Wolfgang produced a sort of divertimento including popular songs, called *Galimathias musicum*. He also wrote a further set of sonatas for publication, dedicated to the Princess of Weilburg. While in The Hague Leopold was delighted to be presented with a copy of his *Violin School*, a fine new edition in Dutch.

The next move was back to Paris, where some of the luggage had been sent direct from Calais. On the way they stopped to give concerts at Amsterdam and Utrecht; then on, by way of Antwerp, Brussels and Cambrai, reaching Paris early in May. This time they stayed only two months, of which several days were spent at Versailles playing before members of the court. Leopold was tempted by the prospect of going on to Italy, but wisely decided against it. It was three years since the travellers had left Salzburg, and now they began their homeward trek in earnest.

But this did not mean taking a direct route if a circuitous one offered better opportunities. So first they went to Dijon, at the request of the Prince of Condé, to play during the triennial meeting of the Burgundian

Leopold Mozart's dedication of a music-book to his son, 1762

estates. A month was spent at Lyons, then a few days each at Geneva, Lausanne, Berne and Zurich, playing to the local connoisseurs. After a brief stop at Schaffhausen they went to the Donaueschingen court, where nine of their twelve evenings were devoted to marathon four-hour concerts before the Prince. Bidding him a tearful farewell, they went through Biberach (where Wolfgang is said to have competed with another prodigy, Sixtus Bachmann), then with short stops at Dillingen and Augsburg to Munich, where they appeared before the Elector. At this point Wolfgang was once more ill, so Leopold dropped his plans for going further afield and took the direct route home.

The family must have been glad, on the 30th of November 1766, to enter Salzburg again—to see the familiar sights and faces, hear the familiar sounds, smell the familiar smells. When they had left, Wolfgang was a small boy of seven-and-a-half, Nannerl a girl of twelve; now he was a growing lad of close on eleven and she was a young lady of fifteen. Leopold resumed his duties at the archiepiscopal court; Frau Mozart and Nannerl resumed their domestic routine; and Wolfgang resumed his studies. And so ended the first grand tour.

Mozart (engraving after the oil painting made in Verona by dalla Rosa, 1770)

Il Maestrino

The fact that the eleven-year-old Wolfgang had a number of compositions to his credit was in itself remarkable. But this should not blind us to the musical weakness and technical inadequacy of these early efforts, which were probably much inferior to his improvisations. Leopold was not so blinded. On returning from the tour he set Wolfgang to work on counterpoint, to give him the facility, discipline and freedom without which no amount of inspiration could be of use.

Accordingly the next ten months were spent in Salzburg—not long, perhaps, to consolidate a contrapuntal technique, but then Wolfgang was somewhat quicker than most students of the subject. During these months he composed several sacred works as well as a dramatic intermezzo in Latin for Salzburg University, called *Apollo et Hyacinthus*, and the first section of an oratorio entitled *Die Schuldigkeit des ersten Gebotes*. (This last was written during a week of confinement at the Archbishop's Residency, to prove to the sceptics that Wolfgang really could compose without his father's help.) The other parts were contributed by Salzburg's two leading composers, Adlgasser and Michael Haydn, Joseph's younger brother. Also from these months are four piano concertos—not original works, but settings for piano and orchestra of movements from sonatas by other composers.

In the autumn of 1767 the Viennese were planning to celebrate the marriage of the King of Naples with the Archduchess Josepha. Here, Leopold thought, was a good opportunity for the profitable exhibition of his children. So in September the family left for the capital. But in Vienna jubilation suddenly changed to mourning, as the bride contracted smallpox and died. The infection was rampant and Leopold was in a dilemma, wanting to take the children away to safety but daily

Pietro Metastasio (engraving by Caronni after Steiner)

expecting a summons to court. When smallpox struck the royal family a second time, the Mozarts promptly departed for Moravia, going first to Brno, then to Olomouc; but there, at the inn, Wolfgang was taken ill —with smallpox. They were now in sore trouble. But it did not last long. Count Podstatzky, dean of the cathedral and a former acquaintance of the Mozarts, showed rare kindness by taking the family into his own home. There Wolfgang recovered from what turned out to be a fairly mild attack and Nannerl had an even milder one. She was left with no pock-marks and Wolfgang with only a few.

Soon they were well enough to return to Vienna, stopping for two weeks at Brno on the journey. They did not find the Viennese atmosphere to their liking. Court appearances were unprofitable, and elsewhere, according to the suspicious Leopold, all the city's composers were doing their best to hamper Wolfgang's advancement (except Wagenseil, who in any case was ill, and Gluck, who was half-hearted). Instead of overcoming the prejudices gradually, Leopold characteristically irritated his opponents by trying to force them into a position where they had to admit the boy's genius. His main scheme was to have an opera by Wolfgang produced at the theatre. The Emperor himself had suggested it: it only remained to carry the plan through.

But it was not so easy. A libretto, *La finta semplice*, was prepared, though sent too late for the proposed performance at Easter 1768. Soon the music was written, but opposition was growing more and more intense. Rumours were set in circulation—that Wolfgang had insufficient knowledge of Italian, that the music was worthless and didn't fit the words, even that it was by Leopold. Leopold offended more susceptibilities by circulating statements by Hasse and Metastasio, Vienna's senior composer and the greatest librettist of the day, that they had seen thirty operas in Vienna worse than Wolfgang's. He even protested to the Emperor himself. In his letters home he wrote lengthily of his and Wolfgang's honour, the reputation of the Salzburg court and the glory of God—and, occasionally, of the hundred-ducat fee which seemed to be eluding his grasp. He only gave up hope of having it staged when the impresario told him frankly that if he persisted a ludicrous failure would be arranged.

The fifteen months in Vienna were not entirely wasted. Wolfgang composed several symphonies, a trumpet concerto (now lost) and a good deal of sacred music, some of it for performance before the Emperor at the dedication of an orphanage. And some compensation for the unperformed Italian opera was afforded by a little German one, *Bastien und Bastienne*, given in a private theatre at the home of the famous Dr. Mesmer, the inventor of magnetism-therapy, who was a friend of the Mozarts.

The family arrived home early in January 1769 with their dignity affronted and their pockets lightened, for the stay in Vienna had been costly and the Archbishop of Salzburg had now quite reasonably decided to stop Leopold's salary during his long periods of absence. Soon after their return the Archbishop ordered a performance of *La finta semplice* at the small theatre in his palace, which must have consoled them for the Viennese disappointments. Wolfgang was now given a post as konzertmeister, apparently honorary at first.

A view of the theatre in the Archbishop's Residency at Salzburg, where 'La finta semplice' was first performed

Abbildung deß Vorderen Theils von dem außgerichteten Theatro in dem Hoch-Fürstl. großen Trabanten Saal.

They were in Salzburg for less than a year. Italy remained to be visited, and here it was not merely a matter of capitalising on the boy's genius while it could still arouse wonder, but a genuine desire to take him to the musical *fons et origo*, to drink of the pristine waters. For Italian music, especially in the all-important field of opera, set the style for most of Europe, and all the greatest German operatic composers (like Handel, Hasse and Gluck) had spent years there perfecting their use of the Italian musical language. The conditions of Italian concert life made it unlikely that the tour would be profitable to the Mozarts. Here they would have to depend largely on individual generosity, as in many towns concerts were only organised by some kind of musical society or patron and were free to members or sometimes eminent citizens.

Wolfgang and Leopold—Nannerl, at eighteen, had outgrown the prodigy stage—set out in December 1769. They had four main stops on the journey. At Innsbruck and Rovereto Wolfgang performed before the local worthies, and he attracted a huge crowd to Rovereto's principal church when he played on the organ there. The same happened at Verona, where they gave a concert which impelled the Veronese poetasters to vie in his praise. At Mantua they were allowed to perform at the musical society's weekly concert: great enthusiasm was aroused by two of Wolfgang's symphonies and his violin and harpsichord playing. Here and at Verona they heard operas, probably by Guglielmi and Hasse.

Arriving in Milan at the end of January 1770, they found pleasantly comfortable lodgings at an Augustinian monastery. An introduction to the Governor-General of Lombardy, Count Firmian, proved very helpful: he organised concerts for them at the homes of the city's leading music-lovers, for which Wolfgang wrote some new arias to demonstrate his powers in dramatic music. They met the veteran composer Giovanni Battista Sammartini, who was amazed by the boy's achievements, and one of Italy's leading operatic composers, Piccini, whose *Cesare in Egitto* they heard at the opera house. In their letters, Leopold and Wolfgang commented little on the actual music they heard; like most eighteenth-century listeners, they seem to have been more interested in the abilities of the individual singers. The important result of the Milan visit was that Wolfgang was commissioned to write an opera for production there at the end of 1770.

After nearly two months in Milan they left for Bologna. On the journey they spent one night at Lodi, where Wolfgang whiled away the evening by writing his first string quartet. They also stopped at Parma, and were invited to dinner by the famous soprano Lucrezia Agujari, who dazzled them with her three-octave range. In Bologna they found as kind a patron in Count Pallavicini as they had at Milan in Count Firmian. Leopold rated the visit as the most successful so far in Italy: Bologna was a scholarly and artistic centre and the audiences there were better judges than most. One outstanding judge was the renowned musical theorist

Padre Martini, who set Wolfgang some exercises in fugue and thoroughly approved of the results. The Mozarts visited another notable musical figure, Farinelli, the greatest of all the castrati.

After a week in Bologna they moved on to Florence, where Wolfgang appeared at court before the Grand Duke. In charge of the musical establishment were the Marchese de Ligniville, an esteemed contrapuntist whose tests Wolfgang worked out with ease, and the violinist Nardini, an old acquaintance from Ludwigsburg. Wolfgang played with Nardini at court. and struck up a close friendship with one of his pupils, an English boy of his own age, Thomas Linley (who unhappily was to die within a few years).

The travellers reached Rome, after a wretched five-day journey, in time for Holy Week. They attended the Sistine Chapel, where Wolfgang performed the prodi-

Padre Giambattista Martini

gious feat of memorising the famous *Miserere* by Allegri and writing it out at home afterwards, checking and correcting his manuscript at a second hearing. Leopold was at first a little anxious over possible official disapproval, as the *Miserere* was sometimes regarded as the Chapel's exclusive property, but in fact the feat provoked only admiration. Arriving with no less than twenty letters of introduction, they appeared at the homes of many of Rome's leading music-lovers, with the usual plaudits—indeed, Leopold wrote home: 'the further we have penetrated into Italy, the greater has been the general amazement'. The Italians, who took it as a matter of course that their nation enjoyed a monopoly of musical genius, were particularly surprised that a youth from across the Alps could show such gifts.

They travelled on to Naples, the furthest point of the tour, after a month's stay in Rome. The King of Naples was apparently something of a Philistine, or so Leopold thought, since he failed to summon Wolfgang to play to him. Nor did the Neapolitans themselves make much impression—Leopold fulminated against their superstitiousness while Wolfgang wondered whether Naples did not surpass even London for the insolence of the people. But they were impressed by the

CAPPELLA PONTIFICCIA.

Filp Juvara del. Roma   J. Caldwall sculp. Londini

beauty of the city itself. They were able to give a public concert, which helped to fill a purse shrinking with disturbing rapidity. During their four weeks there they heard a number of operas, met Paisiello and renewed their acquaintance with Jommelli. Wolfgang was offered an opportunity to write an opera himself for the San Carlo opera house, but had to refuse—as he had done already at Bologna and Rome—on account of the Milan commission.

After a tour to Vesuvius, Pompeii and other sights they left for Rome in mid-June. They had an extremely fast return journey in the mail coach at the cost of an accident which injured Leopold's leg. Back in Rome they were delighted to learn that Wolfgang was to be created a Knight of the Golden Spur by the Pope. This entitled him to be called 'Signor Cavaliere', much to Leopold's amusement. (Several composers received this honour, among them Gluck and Dittersdorf.) Leopold's injury delayed them both at Rome and Bologna, but in the latter city they were at last sent the libretto and list of performers for Wolfgang's new Milan opera. He could now start writing the recitatives, but the arias had to wait until he met the principal singers in Milan, for it was always considered part of the composer's job to acquaint himself with the singers' individual capabilities and provide them with tailor-made music. This may seem strange today, but it was characteristic of the eighteenth century's practical attitude over artistic matters.

During the three months in Bologna father and son met the eminent Bohemian composer Mysliveček, and were called upon by their old London acquaintance Dr. Burney, now on one of his famous musical tours. Shortly before they left Wolfgang was elected to membership of the city's august Accademia Filarmonica, an honour which was normally conferred only on composers of considerable age and experience. He passed the rigorous examination in harmony and counterpoint without difficulty. His original manuscript survives, together with a corrected and improved version by Padre Martini, with whom he had been studying.

Diploma of the Accademia Filarmonica, Bologna, issued to Mozart on 10th October, 1770

Mozart wearing the Order of the Golden Spur (oil painting, 1777)

The travellers reached Milan in mid-October and Wolfgang settled down to work on his new opera, *Mitridate, rè di Ponto*. He soon completed the recitatives, but as the singers were slow in getting to Milan it was impossible to go ahead steadily. And there were various intrigues against him. But eventually all was finished, the malevolent prophets of failure were confounded, and on the 20th of December 1770 the sublimest of operatic composers had his first success in the theatre. Unprecedentedly, there was an encore on the first night, and after almost every aria the theatre echoed to shouts of '*Evviva il maestro! evviva il maestrino!*'. Wolfgang directed the first three of the twenty performances, leaving the rest to Lampugnani and Chiesa. With justified wonder and pride Leopold wrote to his wife:

> 'If about fifteen or eighteen years ago, when Lampugnani had already composed so much in England and Melchior Chiesa in Italy, and I had heard their operas, arias and symphonies, someone had said to me that these masters would take part in the performance of my son's composition, and, when he left the harpsichord, would have to sit down and accompany his music, I should have told him that he was fit for a lunatic asylum.'

A brief excursion took the Mozarts to Turin, then back to Milan, which they finally left at the beginning of February. Passing through Brescia, where they heard an opera, they arrived in Venice in time for the Carnival celebrations. As usual, they played to the local nobility and went to the opera. It was a pleasant month's visit, with plenty of relaxation at the home of a German family, friends of the Hagenauers, where Wolfgang was thoroughly spoiled by the six beautiful daughters.

On the final stages of the journey they spent a day at Padua, playing at two houses and receiving a commission for an oratorio, then a couple of days in Vicenza, at the Bishop's request, and a few in Verona, where Wolfgang had been elected a member of the local Accademia Filarmonica since his last visit. To warm their spirits during the rest of the cold journey home, they found a letter at Verona saying that a serenata was to be commissioned by the Empress Maria Theresa, for performance at royal wedding festivities in Milan the next October.

So when they eventually returned to Salzburg, at the end of March 1771, it was to stay only a few months. Before father and son left again Wolfgang had composed the oratorio for Padua, *La Betulia liberata*, more church music and several symphonies to add to the group he had written in Italy.

Arriving at Milan late in August, Wolfgang soon started work on the serenata, entitled *Ascanio in Alba*. Conditions were less than ideal: he wrote to Nannerl of the fun of composing to the accompaniment of one violinist in the room above, another below, a singing-master in the next room and an oboist opposite—'it gives you plenty of ideas,' he said. Also in Milan was Hasse, writing an opera which was to be the principal entertainment at the celebrations. In the event Wolfgang's serenata was rather better received than Hasse's opera. Leopold wrote home with a blend of anxiety (for Hasse was a powerful figure) and jubilation: 'It really distresses me very greatly, but Wolfgang's serenata has completely killed Hasse's opera.'

The day after Leopold and Wolfgang arrived home, in December 1771, their overlord the Archbishop died. After the easy-going Schrattenbach, the appointment of the reputedly severe Hieronymus, Count of

Colloredo, was not much welcomed by the Salzburgers. For the installation ceremonies Wolfgang was commissioned to write a serenata.

The next few months were particularly prolific. Besides the serenata, *Il sogno di Scipione*, he wrote three fairly extended sacred works, eight symphonies and four divertimentos, of which the instrumental works especially show the strides he was making in musical inventiveness and polish. This stream of compositions may be connected—either as cause or effect, or both—with his receiving his first salaried appointment in August 1772. It was none too liberally salaried, at a mere hundred-and-fifty gulden, but Wolfgang was still only sixteen.

Meanwhile, preparations were under way for a third visit to Italy. After *Mitridate's* success in Milan, Wolfgang had been asked to write another opera, *Lucio Silla*, for production there, so in October he and Leopold set off on the now familiar road. Wolfgang had been sent the libretto in advance and arrived with the recitatives complete: but unfortunately the librettist had sent a copy of his text to Metastasio for approval, and, since the great poet did not entirely approve, several of them had to be rewritten. Then he worked on the choruses and overture, and finally, as the singers began to arrive, on the arias. In the end there was something of a scramble, as the tenor was taken ill and his replacement could not get to Milan until nine days before the performance, but all was ready in time for the first night on the 26th of December.

But even then their troubles were far from over. First, the Archduke remembered that he had to write five letters of New Year greetings before coming, which delayed the start by three hours (he was a slow writer, as Leopold explained); then the stop-gap tenor, a church singer, over-acted and made as if to attack the prima donna, which made the audience laugh; she in turn was disconcerted by the laughter, and still further upset by the applause from the royal box arranged exclusively for himself by the primo uomo. But *Lucio Silla* was a success despite its inauspicious start and was given no less than twenty-six times altogether.

Wolfgang went through the usual round of concerts while in Milan, and he found time to write a motet (*Exsultate, jubilate*) for the primo uomo, Rauzzini, as well as to complete a set of six string quartets which he had started on the journey. But Leopold had nurtured higher hopes from this trip. Fears that Wolfgang's genius would not be adequately recognised and valued by the new Archbishop of Salzburg—and possibly Colloredo had already shown some dislike of the pernickety father and the precocious, opinionated son—led him to look elsewhere for a permanent post for Wolfgang. So he applied to the Grand Duke of Tuscany, in Florence, with Count Firmian's powerful backing. He was kept waiting in Milan until February for an answer: it duly came, and was negative. Possibly the Grand Duke had consulted his mother, Maria Theresa, and received advice similar to that tendered to his brother, the Archduke Ferdinand of Milan, when in 1771 he had considered offering Wolfgang an appointment: 'Don't burden yourself with useless people . . . who drift around like beggars.'

Back in Salzburg from what was to be his last sight of his beloved Italy, Wolfgang busied himself with more composition—symphonies, wind divertimentos, two masses and a two-violin concerto were the main products of the next months. But the restless Leopold was not prepared to stay at home for long. He felt the need to get Wolfgang launched on a respectable and prosperous career and, with his present employer neither well-disposed nor generously inclined, Salzburg seemed an unpromising launching site.

So as soon as the Archbishop was away from Salzburg, and leave of absence could not reasonably be withheld, Leopold and Wolfgang went off to Vienna. The Emperor himself was away during most of their visit, but they appeared at court before Maria Theresa, who was prepared to behave graciously in front of them despite what she had written behind their backs. But it soon became clear that no appointments were to be had in the capital and they returned to Salzburg without gain.

Even if the ten weeks in Vienna were unprofitable in worldly terms, the contact with Viennese music had a far-reaching effect on Wolfgang's development, as we shall see later. The immediate products were six string quartets, and a serenade written for a Salzburg family. During autumn 1773 and most of 1774 he was at home, hard at work on composition—masses, divertimentos, symphonies, his first piano concerto, his first string quintet, his first piano sonatas and, for a Munich amateur, a bassoon concerto. The symphonies include No. 25 in G minor and No. 29 in A, works of a force and personality which must have made evident—if it were not already so—that he was to reach far beyond the horizons of the average eighteenth-century composer.

The routine in Salzburg was agreeably interrupted in December 1774 by a commission from the Elector of Bavaria to write an opera for

A view of Munich (after Canaletto)

production at Munich. Archbishop Colloredo could scarcely refuse permission for father and son to go, and they set off at the beginning of the month. Nannerl came to Munich (after copious instructions from the fussy Leopold about the journey) in time to witness the splendid success of *La finta giardiniera's* first performance, on the 13th of January 1775. It had no spectacular run, like the Milan operas, but that was because the smaller Munich public had to be offered frequent changes of programme or the audiences fell off. The work was soon translated into German and performed by a travelling company in several cities.

Munich's musical court was duly impressed by the opera. Leopold reported that the Archbishop of Salzburg, visiting Munich, was so embarrassed at being congratulated on Wolfgang's achievement that he could only bow his head and shrug his shoulders. The Elector translated his approval into concrete terms by commissioning some church music.

The gay months at the Munich Carnival came to an end all too soon. Leopold and Wolfgang could not absent themselves too long from their stern overlord and they returned to their duties at the Salzburg court and cathedral early in March. Leopold was never to escape, and it was a long two-and-a-half years before Wolfgang was able to set himself free.

A view of the Mirabell Palace, Salzburg

The Fruitless Search

During the events so far described, Mozart's actual personality has remained in the background. We have seen him steered round western Europe, with his father planning every step, dictating every move, and no doubt watching over his progress on every page of every composition. Our only first-hand contact with him (apart, of course, from the music) is in the postscripts to Nannerl on his father's letters home—mainly boyish and high-spirited, with an occasional mysterious message to some Salzburg girl. Not until he was twenty-one did he leave his father's side. We can then see, in his behaviour and from his correspondence, how this upbringing affected him, and we can learn a good deal about the characters of both father and son.

Before Mozart next left Salzburg he had two-and-a-half years of steady work in the Archbishop's service. During this period he produced a vast quantity of music: an opera (*Il rè pastore*) on the occasion of an archduke's visit, serenades for members of the local nobility, violin concertos, piano concertos, church music and arias. But it was not a happy period. Mozart felt cramped and oppressed by the discipline of the Archbishop's exacting regime. Possibly, at the age of twenty, he was becoming anxious to free himself from his father's perpetual domination. He also knew his own abilities, as composer and executant, and he knew that at Salzburg he stood out like a ten-carat diamond in a paste brooch—this was no place for him. Moreover, having seen the courts of half Europe, he had grown impatient with the bourgeois, provincial outlook of the Salzburgers and even rather ashamed of their narrowness. And he wanted more money.

Early in 1777 the Archbishop refused Mozart and his father leave to undertake a tour—why indeed should he pay them for duties which were unperformed while they were away earning money, perhaps even seeking better posts? Eventually the risk had to be taken. During the summer Mozart successfully petitioned the Archbishop for his discharge so that he could travel. Leopold too was offered his discharge, but it would have been exceedingly imprudent to cut off the family's entire income, and the one thing that cannot be said of Leopold is that he was imprudent. It was his prudence which decreed that Mozart should not go travelling on his own. The only person suitable to keep an eye on him was his mother, so in her company he left Salzburg on the 23rd of September.

The tour was, frankly, a hunt for a job. It started in Munich. Mozart was keen on the possibility of settling there with a court appointment, and he had influential friends, notably Count Seeau and the Bishop of Chiemsee, who were able to sound out the position for him with the Elector. At first the Elector excused himself by telling the Bishop that Mozart should study in Italy; then Mozart himself had an audience, at which he pointed out that he had already been to Italy three times and had completed the Bologna Academy test with unprecedented speed. 'Yes, my dear boy,' replied the Elector, 'but I have no vacancy. I am sorry.'

This was the first of many refusals. To us, knowing the extent of his greatness, and that his genius was at least partly discerned in his own time, it may seem incomprehensible that half the potentates of Europe were not pressing him with offers. But the main requirement of a musical establishment at a nobleman's court was that it should function smoothly. It was much more in the interest of an elector or a duke to employ steady, reasonably competent musicians who could be relied upon to carry out instructions and get on with their jobs quietly than to bring in a young genius who was always wanting to go away to write an opera, whose superior ability and arrogant, critical manner would irritate his colleagues, who would probably feel discontent at any but the largest court, and, incidentally, whose music would not seem so very much better than anyone else's.

Leopold was anxious that his son should move on once he was definitely refused an appointment at Munich. But Mozart was in no great hurry. He liked Munich and was loth to leave. He even toyed with an idea put forward by a music-loving innkeeper that ten patrons should be found who would subscribe to his upkeep; this income, together with something from Count Seeau, he thought would be adequate. But Leopold soon poured cold water on his enthusiasm, pointing out how uncertain such a scheme would be. Better hopes sprang from an interview with Mysliveček (now in hospital at Munich with a particularly repulsive illness). The influential Bohemian felt a genuine affection and admiration for Mozart and asked some friends at Naples to obtain an

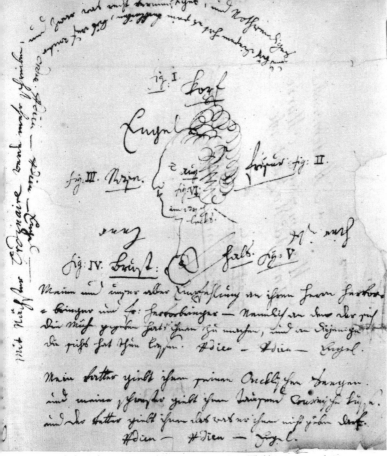

Part of a letter from Mozart to his cousin, Maria Anna Thekla Mozart, 10th May, 1779

opera commission for him. The plan came to nothing; it merely aroused in Mozart what he described as an 'inexpressible longing' to write operas again.

They eventually moved on to Augsburg, where Mozart struck up a playful, flirtatious friendship with his cousin Maria Anna Thekla Mozart, the daughter of Leopold's youngest brother. Romantic biographers have been much troubled by the bathroom humour in Mozart's letters to her (and in some of his mother's letters home). But it was simply the normal humour of a period in which the body and its natural functions did not have to be spoken of in hushed tones, and does not need to be taken too seriously. While in Augsburg Mozart gave a successful public concert with the poor local orchestra and a private concert to a group of local 'patricians'; he also made the acquaintance of Stein, one of the leading piano-makers of the time.

Leopold urged him to move on quickly to various cities where there were courts, particularly to those without too Italianate an outlook. So on the way to Mannheim he called at Hohenaltheim, where the court of the Prince Oettingen-Wallerstein was situated. Unfortunately, the Prince was in a state of deep melancholy—Mozart's mother wrote that he could not look at anybody without bursting into tears—and was in no mood to offer patronage. There Mozart met the composer Antonio Rosetti (a Czech who had Italianised his name) and the keyboard virtuoso von Beecke, with whom he had often been compared. It seems, from tales which reached Salzburg, that he behaved with childish frivolity one evening at Hohenaltheim, providing his enemies with ample material for malicious gossip.

They arrived at Mannheim on the 30th of October 1777. Mozart soon made friends among the excellent musicians of the famous orchestra. He spent much of his time at the home of Cannabich, the orchestra's director, helping his thirteen-year-old daughter Rosa with her piano playing and writing a sonata for her. Among his other friends at Mannheim were the kapellmeister, Holzbauer, the well-known but ageing tenor, Raaff, the oboist, Ramm, and the flautist, Wendling, whose wife was a fine soprano and whose daughter had just become an ex-mistress of the Elector. He made a few enemies, too, among them the vice-kapellmeister Abbé Vogler and Peter von Winter.

The court showed little Italian influence. Formerly it had been somewhat French in outlook, but by now it was under the sway of strong German national feeling. While Mozart was there he saw Holzbauer's German opera *Günther von Schwarzburg*, and he met the great poet Wieland, visiting Mannheim to work on a German opera with the rather inferior composer Schweitzer. Mozart gave a concert with the orchestra and met the Elector, who seemed friendly and appreciative. For playing to the Elector and advising about the teaching of his children he was given a watch—his fifth, he mentioned in a letter to Leopold, recording his intention of wearing two at once in future so as to avert the possibility of receiving a sixth. His hopes of a permanent or even a temporary appointment were high. It was not until he had been in Mannheim some six weeks that he finally heard that the Elector had nothing to offer.

He was acutely disappointed by the decision, and his friends were highly indignant. It was by now mid-December, no time of year for travelling on, so Cannabich and Wendling arranged for him to take a few pupils, obtained some commissions (for flute quartets and concertos) and helped him to find cheaper lodgings. (In fact, owing largely to Mozart's own laziness, the commissions were never completed; nor were they fully paid for.) In the spring, it was decided, he would go on to Paris with Wendling, Ramm and the bassoonist Ritter, his mother returning home.

Meanwhile Leopold, at home in Salzburg, was desperate with anxiety.

Aloysia Weber, in the costume of Zémire from the opera 'Zémire et Azor' by Grétry (engraving by Nilson)

Most of the letters he was receiving were cheerful to the point of frivolity, although the tour was so far a dismal failure. He was infuriated by the carelessness of his son and wife, their irresponsibility with money, their slackness in keeping him informed of their plans, their dilatory progress, their foolishness in contemplating impracticable, unprofitable projects and in travelling without proper letters of introduction or credit. He wrote lengthy screeds of advice, about possible routes, various plans of campaign, ways of handling people so as to get the greatest possible amount of money from them, and so on. There is something deeply pathetic in the thought of the perpetually worried Leopold, performing his arduous duties at Salzburg, sitting there in his old, fraying clothes, eating frugally, perhaps playing a little music with Nannerl in the evenings, and constantly racking his brains to devise elaborate schemes on Wolfgang's behalf to divert his colossal genius into useful and profitable channels.

It was at this time that Mozart first fell in love. Among his Mannheim acquaintances were the Weber family: the father was a music copyist and the second daughter, Aloysia, a girl of about seventeen, was a fine soprano singer. It was his love for Aloysia which made him take an otherwise pointless few days' trip to Kircheim-Bolanden, with her and her father, to perform there before the Princess of Weilburg; it was his love for Aloysia which led him to madden Leopold with the fatuous suggestion that he should tour Italy with the Webers, to compose for Aloysia, who overnight would turn into a prima donna; and it was his love for Aloysia that led him to cancel his journey to Paris with the three Mannheim musicians who, he suddenly convinced himself, were too irreligious to be suitable travelling companions.

Leopold was driven almost frantic by Wolfgang's latest ideas. In a long, angry but perfectly reasonable letter, he pointed out the utter stupidity of his latest suggestions. He urged him: '*Off with you to Paris!* and that soon! Find your place among great people. *Aut Caesar aut nihil.*' He ended by saying that his mother was to accompany him to Paris, not to return home as planned; clearly he felt that Wolfgang had hardly shown himself fit to travel alone.

Mozart and his mother duly left for Paris in mid-March, armed with a host of instructions from Leopold as to what was to be done, what was not to be done, who was to be seen, who was to be avoided. On arrival they contacted Baron Grimm, who had helped them on their previous

Title-page of the
first edition of the
'Paris' Symphony

visits. Another useful friend was the Palatinate Ambassador, Count von Sickingen. Mozart soon met the director of the famous Concert Spirituel, Le Gros, who promptly commissioned some replacement movements for a Holzbauer *Miserere*—which were only partly performed and are now lost. A more promising venture was a Sinfonia Concertante for Wendling, Ramm, Ritter and the hornist Punto, but owing to some intrigue (possibly on the part of Cambini, whom Mozart had foolishly alienated) the work was suppressed and again may be lost.

Meanwhile, Mozart was making himself known by calling on potential patrons and playing to them—though it seems that his manner on such occasions was sometimes less deferential than was expected of him. He also undertook some teaching, rather unwillingly, for he disliked the drudgery and was all too ready to give up a pupil (and her fee) if she was out when he called or was insufficiently talented. One of his pupils was the daughter of the Duc de Guines, for whom the flute and harp Concerto was written. Some fascinating information on his teaching methods is contained in one of his letters about her.

It was an unfortunate time to be in Paris. The famous paper war between the supporters of Gluck and those of Piccini was at its height and this was hardly the moment for a visiting young musician to make his mark. Mozart might have made more impression had his plans to write an opera for Paris materialised. As it was, the Parisians did not hear much of his music. A couple of symphonies (including the *Paris*) and a ballet, *Les petits riens*, were the main works with which he appeared before the French public: otherwise his only compositions there were a few sonatas and some variations on French songs, no doubt designed to divert the noble families upon whom he called.

At one time the quest for a permanent post seemed to be over, when Mozart was offered an organist's appointment at Versailles. The pay was quite good and the duties moderate, for he was required only six months of the year. But he refused the offer, partly because he disliked Paris, the Parisians and French music in general, and partly because he was unwilling to accept anything less than a full kapellmeistership—a post for which he knew he was entirely fitted but which, as Leopold pointed out, he could hardly expect at the age of twenty-two.

While Mozart was enjoying the prolonged freedom from the pettiness and tyranny of Salzburg, his mother must have felt sad at being so far from her home, her husband and her daughter. She found it hard enough to cope with the problems of food and lodgings, let alone to look after Wolfgang. In a private note to Leopold which she once surreptitiously added to a letter home (in her mis-spelt, ungrammatical style) she wrote that Wolfgang would never listen to her remonstrances, that she was worried by his impetuousness and his desire to 'give up his life and property' for anyone he liked—referring, of course, to the Webers.

The chapel at Versailles, where Mozart was offered an organist's appointment

Health, in those insanitary days, was always an important topic in her letters. On the 12th of June 1778 she wrote from Paris that she and Wolfgang were well. It was her last letter: in three weeks she was dead. A few days after undergoing the routine procedure of being bled, on the 11th, she contracted some kind of fever. Her condition steadily worsened; the usual family remedies, for what they were worth, made no difference; an aged German doctor living in Paris could not help; Grimm's doctor was equally useless; and after delirium and finally deafness she died on the 3rd of July.

With the consolation of a firm religious faith, and much else to occupy his lively mind, Mozart came through the ordeal resiliently. The immediate problem was to inform Leopold, as yet ignorant of his wife's illness, of the tragedy. So Mozart wrote to him, saying only that she was gravely ill. Recovery from serious illness was rare, and as he read the letter Leopold feared the worst. His fears were soon confirmed when a close family friend, Abbé Bullinger, called. He had just received a letter from Mozart, written at the same time as the letter to Leopold, and came to break the sad news as gently as possible.

So now Mozart was alone in Paris. With his pupils away for the summer and no major commissions, he was not very busy. He had a welcome opportunity to renew his old friendship with J. C. Bach, over from London to hear the Parisian singers before writing an opera for them. During July Baron Grimm, with whom Mozart was staying, wrote a frank letter to Leopold telling him that Wolfgang's prospects in Paris were poor: his visit was ill-timed because of the Gluck-Piccini controversy, and he was not prepared to take enough trouble to make himself known—he would do better with half the talent and double the worldly wisdom. Relations between Mozart and Grimm were by this time deteriorating, partly through Mozart's reluctance to side firmly

Mozart's mother (engraving after [?] Lorenzoni)

Ignaz von Beecke   *Franz Anton Rosetti*

with Piccini in the operatic controversies, partly because Grimm was anxious about the repayment of some money he had lent Mozart, and partly, it would appear, because Mozart reacted in the normal way of someone feeling an irksome obligation.

With Paris evidently having nothing more to offer, opportunities had to be sought elsewhere. Mozart was keen to try Munich: the previous Elector had just died and the Elector of the Palatinate had succeeded him, abandoning the Mannheim court and taking most of his musicians, including the Webers, to the Bavarian capital. Mainz was another possibility, but a remote one—to Leopold's annoyance, Mozart had neglected to visit the court there when he had been nearby at Mannheim.

But while Munich and Mainz offered mere hopes, Salzburg now offered certainty. During Mozart's absence the situation had changed, as two of the senior musicians had died. After exercising considerable diplomacy, Leopold had succeeded in procuring from the Archbishop not only the offer of a much better post but also an apology for his previous cavalier treatment of Mozart. But Mozart remained strongly averse to the idea of returning to the archiepiscopal, and perhaps the parental, yoke; he did not want a menial post and tried to lay down conditions under which he would return. Leopold was able to reassure him: he would be organist and konzertmeister, with a much increased status and responsibility. Moreover, he would be allowed to travel,

Josef Mysliveček   *Ignaz Jakob Holzbauer*

Leopold would at last receive a kapellmeister's appointment, and
(Leopold pointed out) in the not unlikely event of a soprano being
required Aloysia Weber might well be considered. And the combined
salaries of father and son would be enough to remedy the sadly depressed state of the family finances.

Mozart could not refuse. But at the last moment he wanted to prolong
his stay in Paris, to collect fees, correct proofs and even embark on a set
of trios for publication; indeed, after his departure, he rather unkindly
told Leopold that it was only for the family's sake that he had given up
hopes of making his fortune in the French capital. Leaving eventually at
the end of September 1778, he travelled by an exceptionally slow coach
—Grimm had made the arrangements—through Nancy to Strasburg.
There he gave a successful solo concert, then a concert to a practically
empty theatre and a third one when floods made it impossible for him
to leave.

He then made something of a detour so as to visit his 'beloved
Mannheim', where Mme. Cannabich and many other friends received
him kindly. There he heard a 'duodrama' by Georg Benda, a new kind
of dramatic composition consisting of recitation with a musical background; he started to write one himself, as well as a double concerto
for violin and piano, but neither was finished. Meanwhile, Leopold
was enraged by the slowness of his son's homeward journey. While
Mozart was dawdling at Strasburg and Mannheim, not troubling to

keep his father informed of his progress (or lack of it), Leopold was apprehensive that the Archbishop would grow tired of waiting for his dilatory employee and cancel the appointment. So after another irate letter from home Mozart left Mannheim, early in December.

Arriving in Munich, he at once went to the Webers, armed with a fine new aria for Aloysia. But he met with a bitter disappointment. Looking forward to a loving reunion—perhaps even an early marriage —with Aloysia, he found her altogether changed. With a lucrative court appointment, she no longer needed Mozart's help or the advice which he had proffered with a liberality quite inappropriate to his own uncertain position. Her greeting was friendly but cool. Mozart was deeply depressed. He hung on in Munich for a few days, waiting to present the Electress with a copy of a newly published set of sonatas which he had dedicated to her. Thoughts of a possible lukewarm reception at home were worrying him, too, for Leopold's recent letters had been at best cold and often heated. But he soon had reassurances on that score, through a family friend in Munich.

So in the middle of January 1779 Mozart left for Salzburg, finally abandoning the long, wearisome and altogether fruitless search for a good appointment. His homecoming could not have been an entirely happy occasion. Relations between Mozart and his father had undergone a good deal of strain over the last few months: Mozart may well have felt that he had been tricked into returning to servitude, while Leopold clearly thought his son deficient in sense of duty. The tour had not merely been a failure; it had also embodied tragedy, in the death of Mozart's mother. However, the family were glad to be reunited and celebrated the occasion by giving the prodigal son his favourite dish, roast capons.

Georg Benda

J. W. A. Stamitz

Hieronymus, Count Colloredo, Archbishop of Salzburg (oil painting by König)

Servitude and Freedom

It is not hard to imagine Mozart's feelings as he took up his duties at Salzburg. During the last few months he had buried his mother, he had been rejected by his beloved and he had signally failed to improve his worldly position. Although very much aware of his superlative musical gifts, he had a sense of personal inferiority (so common in men of very small stature), which comes out all too clearly in his arrogance, his constant desire to outshine his rivals, his craving for close friends, and in many other ways. It must have been aggravated by the humiliation of having to return to irksome duties in a town he despised and under a master he hated.

Little happened in the course of the next two years to disturb the routine of Mozart's life. He carried out his ordinary duties and composed what was required of him, including church music and symphonies. But dramatic music remained closest to his heart. He started work on a German comic opera, *Zaïde*, which was never completed, and wrote some incidental music to *König Thamos* for a visiting theatrical company under Emanuel Schikaneder. Then a real opportunity arose. In 1780 a commission came from the Bavarian Elector for an opera to be given in Munich at the 1781 Carnival celebrations. The chosen subject was *Idomeneo*, and a Salzburg cleric, Varesco, was commissioned to adapt the libretto from an earlier French version. Archbishop Colloredo made some difficulties but could not ultimately refuse permission for his employee to go to Munich at the Elector's command.

Mozart left Salzburg in November 1780, with much of his score already written, for he knew three of the performers well and could write their music at home. (The Weber family, incidentally, had by this time left Munich for Vienna.) Apart from the Wendling sisters-in-law, the singers gave Mozart a good deal of trouble. Raaff's vocal powers had waned, but his *amour propre* had not, while his acting ability remained as it always had been—precisely nil. Mozart had to exercise all his tact and ingenuity to keep the vain old man content. The castrato, del Prato, had not even the remnants of a voice and as an actor was comparable only with Raaff.

The first performance of *Idomeneo* had to be postponed until the end of January 1781 owing to the death of the Empress Maria Theresa. Leopold and Nannerl came over to Munich for it, and in consequence Mozart provided no written account of the opera's reception. But if one may judge from the success of the rehearsals, the performance itself must have been a major triumph. Mozart, who had been troubled by a severe cold all through the preparations for *Idomeneo*, took advantage of the Archbishop's temporary absence from Salzburg and stayed on in Munich for the Carnival festivities, into which he threw himself with considerable gusto.

Then came a shock. A message arrived from the Archbishop, visiting Vienna with part of his court, peremptorily summoning Mozart to join him. Having to leave his Munich friends so soon after a brief taste of success and freedom, it is hardly surprising that he arrived in Vienna in a rebellious frame of mind. Nor is it surprising that he was bitterly indignant to find himself treated as little better than a lackey at Colloredo's Viennese establishment, where he had to eat along with the cooks and valets.

His conduct in the next few weeks is not difficult to understand. One evening he was directed to attend with the Archbishop's entourage at Prince Galitzin's house: instead of presenting himself to the valet as instructed he simply walked in and conversed with the Prince, whom he knew, much to the Archbishop's annoyance. Then Colloredo refused him permission to play at a charity concert, but had to give way in response to outside pressure. Next Mozart was refused permission to give a concert of his own. Meanwhile, he had to play at musical evenings at the Archbishop's residence; he was infuriated by Colloredo's meanness on these occasions, especially as one of them had prevented him from appearing before the Emperor at Count Thun's house, where each of the players had been rewarded with fifty ducats—just half Mozart's annual salary.

Naturally enough, Mozart now began to consider seriously the idea of leaving the Archbishop's service. His recent successes and the promise of an opportunity to write a German opera in Vienna made him confident that he could do far better in the capital than in Salzburg. Matters came to a head over a trivial point, the date on which Mozart was to leave for home. He wanted to stay in Vienna a few days longer to collect some payments due to him, but the Archbishop required him to leave at once, taking charge of a parcel. Mozart refused, and as he was now living at his own expense (having just left the Archbishop's residence for the Webers' house) he had a good case. But Colloredo was furious, and showered him with abuse hardly of archiepiscopal dignity. Mozart resigned on the spot, and confirmed it in writing. But it seems that the Archbishop was unwilling to let him go. One of the court attendants, Count Arco, tried to bring about a reconciliation and refused his resignation on the grounds that Leopold would not consent to it. Then Mozart heard that the Archbishop was about to leave, with the resignation still not accepted. So he demanded another interview with him, but instead was seen by Arco. Tempers evidently became frayed, for this encounter ended with the decisive and celebrated placing of Arco's boot on Mozart's behind.

Mozart's account of all these happenings in his letters home makes it clear how badly he felt he had been used. Leopold, always ready to believe the worst of his son, was unconvinced, but Mozart's biographers have usually been willing to accept his story as it stands. Certainly, he was not treated with the respect nowadays accorded to genius. But even if Colloredo and eventually Arco were inclined to be harsh, one should realise that Mozart must have seemed to them a conceited, wilful and recalcitrant young puppy who only made it difficult to keep the court's musical activities running smoothly. They must have known that he was

A view of the Graben, Vienna; Mozart lived in this square from September 1781 to July 1782, and again during part of 1784

Ansicht vom Graben gegen den Kohlmarkt.

Vue du Graben vers le Kohlmarkt.

A scene from 'The Seragli

Glyndebourne

Muzio Clementi

abnormally gifted, but could scarcely have comprehended the scope of his genius; and even if they could have done, it was hardly their duty to nurture it at their own extreme inconvenience. The fact that Colloredo did not dismiss Leopold, or in any way victimise him, suggests that he was not quite as odious a character as Mozart claimed or Leopold feared.

Now on his own in Vienna, Mozart calculated that with his one pupil (charging her a high fee, to make people realise his worth) he could make a living, with concert appearances and the projected opera to help. The historic kick had been administered on the 9th of June, by which time Mozart had already been staying with the Webers for a month. Aloysia was now married and her father was dead, so the family comprised only the mother and three daughters. During July rumours began to circulate to the effect that Mozart was to marry one of the girls, Constanze, another soprano but not of Aloysia's calibre. Mozart indignantly denied it in a letter home: 'If ever there was a time when I thought less of getting married, it is most certainly now ! . . . I have nothing against matrimony, but at the moment it would be a misfortune for me. . . . Besides, I am not in love with her.'

In the late summer and autumn Mozart worked steadily on his new opera, *Die Entführung aus dem Serail* (*The Seraglio*). He had hoped for the distinction of having it performed during the Russian Grand Duke's visit to Vienna, but in the event precedence was given to works by Gluck. Even so, he was recognised in court circles to the extent of being asked to perform before the visiting Duke of Wurtemburg, and he may also have played to the Grand Duke.

But the most important event of the latter part of 1781 was Mozart's *volte face* on the question of marrying Constanze Weber. In the summer, nothing had been further from his thoughts; by December he was asking his father's consent to the marriage. He had managed to convince himself, despite his earlier ideas on the folly of 'saddling himself with a wife', that two could live even more cheaply than one. In a letter home he told Leopold how great an advantage it would be to have a wife, to look after his clothes and belongings and to satisfy the strong sexual side of his nature, which he had never indulged. He went on to describe the members of the Weber family, all of them unpleasant in various ways apart from Constanze, the family martyr, who alone was kind and clever.

He had reason to know of the unpleasantness of the Webers. The mother was a lazy, cunning woman, overfond of strong drink, who must have been thoroughly delighted by the success of the trap she had laid for Mozart. It was she, no doubt, who had inspired the rumours about him and Constanze (though she had affected to try to scotch them). An old enemy of Mozart's from Mannheim, Peter von Winter, had suggested to Constanze's guardian that Mozart had been over-friendly with the girl and that she would be 'ruined'. The guardian thereupon forbade Mozart to see Constanze unless he signed a document promising to marry her within three years or to compensate her handsomely. There was clearly no honourable alternative, and the document was signed. That Constanze, with a theatrical gesture, tore it up, made no

Mozart's mother-in-law,
Cäcilia Weber

Title-page of the first edition of 'The Seraglio'

difference—except to assure Mozart of her innate goodness and to increase his determination to marry her as soon as possible. So when he proclaimed how much he loved his Constanze, and what a fine wife she would make him, he was probably to some extent deceiving himself into making the best of the situation.

Meanwhile, his life moved in a steady routine, which he described as follows: he was woken at 6 o'clock, dressed by 7, then he composed till 9 or 10, when he went out to give daily one-hour lessons to his pupils, of whom he then had two or three. He lunched at 2 or 3 and, unless he was at a concert, worked steadily at composition from 5 or 6 until 9. Then he went to see Constanze, arriving home at half past 10 or 11 and settling down to more composition, sometimes until 1. That, at any rate, was the programme; to what extent he adhered to it can only be conjectured. With three pupils, he calculated, each paying him six ducats a month, he should have a secure income about double his former salary in Salzburg, and in Vienna he could augment this by publishing his music and playing at concerts. There was also the prospect of occasional appearances at court, which were well rewarded (as when

Caterina Cavalieri,
the first Constanze
in 'The Seraglio'

he appeared with the famous pianist Muzio Clementi—whom he after-wards described as a 'mere mechanicus'). Most of his working time was spent on *The Seraglio*, but he also wrote some serenades, a new finale for his first piano concerto and some fugues—his sudden interest in this old-fashioned form had been sparked off by Baron Gottfried van Swieten, who gave regular Sunday concerts including music by such forgotten masters as J. S. Bach and Handel.

After many delays—some Mozart's fault, some due to intrigues—*The Seraglio* was eventually performed in July 1782. A little organised

Valentin Adamberger,
the first Belmonte
in 'The Seraglio'

hissing hardly marred its success. 'Vienna refuses to hear anything else,' Mozart wrote to his father, and the Emperor, though he thought it had 'too many notes', approved of it. It had about twenty performances in Vienna and was soon staged in many other centres, such as Prague, Frankfurt and Leipzig.

But during his success Mozart was beset with personal worries. The position at the Weber home had become intolerable; the only solution was for Mozart and Constanze to marry at once. Mozart, though of course he did not need it, wanted his father's consent. Leopold seems to have been in a disgruntled mood. He replied coldly to the news of *Seraglio's* success, said he had had no time even to unpack the score Mozart had sent, and merely proffered useless advice. On the 4th of August, to the accompaniment of much weeping, Mozart and Constanze were married—and the next day Leopold's grudging consent arrived.

Part of Mozart's marriage contract, showing the seals and signatures of Mozart, his wife, his mother-in-law and three witnesses

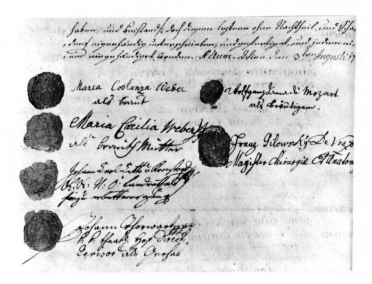

Triumphs and Poverty

Mozart and Constanze settled down to a more or less happy marriage. She was not a person of great intelligence or personality; her self-conscious attempts to write friendly letters to Leopold and Nannerl are almost pathetic, and she was often thoughtless (for example, Mozart was once much distressed during their engagement by her joining in a game where a young man measured her calves). But she was generally an adequate wife and the couple had an easy-going and affectionate relationship.

Unfortunately, she does not seem to have been a very frugal housekeeper. Before the marriage, Mozart once wrote to Leopold: 'It is a downright lie that she is inclined to be extravagant.' Perhaps he later found that the rumours of her extravagance which Leopold had evidently heard were in fact justified, for the young couple were congenitally short of money. Even in the first few years of their marriage, when he was perpetually busy with pupils and concerts, they seem to have lived something of a hand-to-mouth existence, often moving from one apartment to another, better or worse as their finances waxed or waned. Indeed, they waned within six months of marriage to such an extent that Mozart was forced to borrow. At this time he toyed with the idea of settling in Paris or even London, but Leopold, having consulted a Viennese friend and been assured that prospects there were reasonable, advised against it.

This was a prolific period: perhaps the cessation of pre-marital tensions and anxieties released his creative energy. By July 1783 he had written three piano concertos for publication, two horn concertos, some piano music, most of a mass, which he had vowed to write for Constanze but never in fact completed, and the first three of a set of string quartets to be dedicated to Haydn (he had met the elder master, who occasionally visited Vienna, in 1781). The impassioned minuet of the second quartet, in D minor, was composed while Constanze was in labour—their first child, a boy, was born in June.

Relations between Mozart and his father were still not ideal. Leopold was clearly annoyed by some of the stories he heard of his son's boastfulness and irresponsibility, and he was far from pleased by the marriage. Mozart was just as clearly annoyed by his father's ready belief in such stories and by his frequent reproaches; it is not hard to detect the note of petulance that crept into his letters around 1782. Another sore point was the proposed visit of Mozart and Constanze to Salzburg. It had to be postponed time after time—first through the beginning of the Viennese season, then because Mozart's pupils were unwilling to forgo lessons while he was away, then because of the imminence of Constanze's confinement. And even then Mozart was hesitant as he was afraid that the Archbishop could arrest him. Leopold, who had yet to meet his daughter-in-law, called the series of postponements 'mere humbug' and doubted whether they really wanted to visit him at all. When the baby was christened Raimund Leopold he was further displeased at having his own name placed second to that of the other godfather, Baron Raimund Wetzlar, a wealthy Jewish merchant who had helped Mozart generously.

Mozart and Constanze finally departed for Salzburg at the end of July and stayed for three months, during which their baby, left in Vienna with a foster-mother, died. It was no mere holiday at Salzburg: while he was there Mozart composed two violin and viola duets for Michael Haydn, who had been ill and was unable to complete a commission from the Archbishop, and set parts of two weak librettos for Italian operas, which he soon abandoned. Another by-product of the trip was the *Linz* Symphony. On the return journey to Vienna in the autumn, they spent a few days at Linz with relatives of a Viennese acquaintance, Count Thun. Mozart gave a concert there, writing to Leopold: 'As I have not a single symphony with me, I am writing a new one at breakneck speed' (an excellent example of the workmanlike spirit of the time: he did not sit and wait for the unpredictable Muse to supply him with inspiration but simply got down to the job). His programme at Linz also included a symphony by Michael Haydn, to which he added a brief slow introduction; this work has mistakenly been included among Mozart's own symphonies as No. 37.

The next period of Mozart's life was perhaps his happiest, his most successful and one of his most prolific. A steady flow of pupils during 1784 kept him busy and as financially stable as he ever managed to be, while concerts, at the houses of various noblemen and in public, increased his already fast-growing reputation. He organised some concerts himself, a series of three by subscription and two public ones in the theatre. In a letter home he listed his engagements over one hectic

Constanze Mozart (oil painting by Lange, 1782)

month, including a spell of eleven days with ten concerts. Yet during this frantically busy period he found time to produce masterpieces, among them several piano concertos, a piano and wind quintet and a piano and violin sonata—this last composed in such haste that by the first performance he had not even written out the piano part and had to play it from memory. Later in this *annus mirabilis* he added two more piano concertos, some solo piano music and a string quartet.

At the end of 1784 Mozart became a freemason. Though still a more or less orthodox Catholic, he was much attracted by the ferment of liberal ideas in Viennese intellectual circles, on such subjects as freedom of conscience and universal brotherhood. Freemasonry was later to have far-reaching effects on his music, especially *The Magic Flute*, but as early as 1784 he composed works to be performed by his fellow masons, among them songs, a cantata and some wind music. The deeply-felt Funeral Music for two brother masons was written the next year.

Early in 1785 Mozart persuaded his father to come and visit him in Vienna. Leopold must indeed have wondered at what he saw and heard. He must certainly have felt that his son had 'made good'. In enthusiastic, even slightly bewildered terms he wrote to Nannerl (now Baroness von Sonnenburg—she had married the previous summer) about his son's splendid apartments, at a rent slightly more than the entire salary he had received in Salzburg; he told her of the 'rush and bustle' of Mozart's life, with teaching, composing and almost daily concerts; he

Title-page of the first edition of the masonic cantata 'Die Maurerfreude'

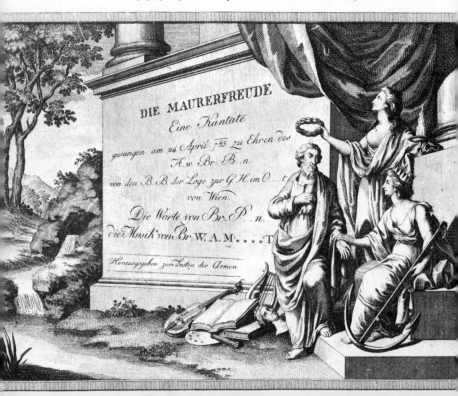

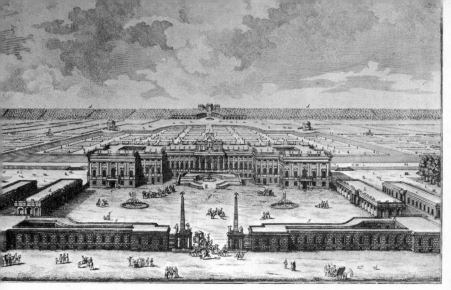

A view of Schönbrunn Palace, Vienna, where 'The Impresario' was first performed

described some of the performances, mentioning how during one of his son's piano concertos 'I had the great pleasure of hearing so clearly all the interplay of the instruments that for sheer delight tears came into my eyes.' Perhaps what impressed him most was a meeting with Joseph Haydn, who came up to Mozart's apartment one evening for a play-through of the newly finished set of six quartets which Mozart had dedicated to him. 'Before God and as an honest man,' Haydn told Leopold, 'I tell you that your son is the greatest composer known to me either in person or by name. He has taste and, what is more, the most profound knowledge of composition.' The aging Leopold must have returned home well contented.

By now, with all his concerts, his pupils and his publications, Mozart should have been prospering. But in fact he was in debt and having to borrow from friends. One can only suppose that he must have spent money as freely as he took it—all our knowledge of his personality suggests that he was the sort of man who liked to impress his friends with exhibitions of open-handed generosity. He and Constanze certainly had many friends and a full social life. Among their intimates were the intellectual Jacquin family, Aloysia Lange (née Weber) and her artist husband, and a small British group of musicians: two composers who took lessons with Mozart, Thomas Attwood and Stephen Storace, Storace's sister Nancy, an excellent singer, and the Irish tenor Michael Kelly, with whom Mozart often played billiards and drank punch. Stories of Mozart's excesses, carnal as well as bibulous, were grossly exaggerated by his early biographers at a time when such failings were considered an ineluctable part of a true artist's make-up. Even so, it does seem that some of his near-priggish moral strictness disappeared, or at least declined, after his marriage.

In autumn 1785 Mozart at last started work in earnest on a new opera. The libretto was by Lorenzo da Ponte, a priest-cum-adventurer-cum-poet of Venetian Jewish origin, and was based on Beaumarchais' political satire *Le Mariage de Figaro*, a sequel to his *Le Barbier de Séville*, of which Paisiello's operatic version was extremely popular. (Mozart had renewed his old acquaintance with Paisiello the previous year—in fact he had caught rheumatic fever at a performance of one of his operas.) He worked steadily on da Ponte's text at the end of the year and in the early months of 1786, taking time off to write music for immediate use at concerts, including a piano quartet and three more magnificent piano concertos, among them the popular A major and C minor. Another product of these months was *Der Schauspieldirektor* (*The Impresario*), a one-act operetta commissioned for performance at Schönbrunn, along with one in Italian by the court composer, Salieri, in honour of a visit by the Governor-General of the Netherlands.

There was some difficulty in getting *Le nozze di Figaro* staged, owing to intrigues by the composers Salieri and Righini, each with his own

A scene from 'Figaro' at Glyndebourne

Nancy Storace, the first Susanna in 'Figaro'

Pierre Caron de Beaumarchais (from a pastel by Perronneau)

opera awaiting production, and the librettist Casti. At one time Mozart is said to have threatened to destroy his score if there were any more postponements. The first performance eventually took place on the 1st of May 1786. So many encores were given on the first night that the work took almost double the appointed time, but even so it had only nine performances during its eight months in the repertory.

Figaro brought Mozart little profit. In the following months he struggled to think up ways of making more money. The impending departure of his British friends even led him to consider a journey to London, but when Leopold indignantly refused to look after the children in their absence the idea had to be dropped. Despite all his worries, the latter part of 1786 saw another of Mozart's great creative spells—six splendid chamber works, a horn concerto, a piano concerto and the *Prague* Symphony were all written within six months.

The symphony was composed for a visit at the beginning of 1787 to the Bohemian capital, where Mozart's reputation already stood high. *Seraglio* had been a success there four years earlier and now the city was mad with enthusiasm over *Figaro*. He wrote with delight to Jacquin of a fashionable ball where the pretty women danced to his *Figaro* music, arranged as contradances and German dances: 'They talk of nothing but *Figaro*; nothing is played, sung or whistled but *Figaro*; no opera is drawing like *Figaro*; nothing, nothing but *Figaro*'—*Figaro* here, *Figaro* there, indeed! Going to hear it at the Prague Opera House, he received a tremendous ovation and was invited to conduct another performance a few days later. It was at the opera house too that he gave his concert, including the new symphony. His successes put him in high spirits, and he chatted so much during a Paisiello opera that he could not tell Jacquin whether the singing was good or bad.

Mozart's friends in Prague included the Duschek family, old Salzburg acquaintances, and Count Thun. It was probably through these influential people that he had the pleasant prospect of a second visit in the autumn, as he had been commissioned to write a new opera for production there. On his return to Vienna in February he at once went to ask da Ponte for a libretto. Although the effervescent abbate was currently working on texts for Salieri and Martín y Soler, he consented and suggested the subject of Don Juan, with which he must have felt a certain amount of natural sympathy. As he embarked on the composition of *Don Giovanni*, the thirty-one-year-old Mozart moved into the final stage of his creative career.

The first page of the thematic catalogue which Mozart started keeping in 1784; the works shown are four piano concertos (K.449–51 and 453) and the Quintet for piano and wind instruments (K.452)

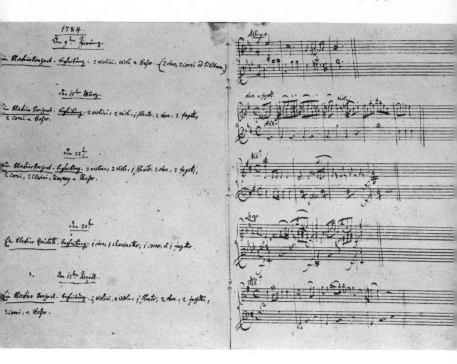

Letter from Mozart to his sister, 19th December, 1787

The Closing Years

The story of Mozart's last four years is an unhappy one, a story of desperate struggles through illness and ever-deepening debt, culminating in his death at the age of thirty-five. He had a sharp reminder of human mortality during 1787. In April he heard that his father was ill, and at the end of May news came of his death. As a sincere freemason, Mozart saw death as 'the best and truest friend of mankind'; his views are movingly set out in the last surviving letter to his father, written on hearing of his illness. Mozart's serene and resigned attitude to death undoubtedly coloured the music of his last years, and it is arguable that his own end was hastened by his ready, even willing, acknowledgment of its inevitability.

Much of the spring and summer of 1787 was spent in the composition of *Don Giovanni*. But in the weeks of his father's last illness he produced two of his most profound chamber works (the string quintets in C and G minor), and later in the summer he composed his greatest violin sonata, the serenade *Eine Kleine Nachtmusik* and several songs. It was during this year that Mozart was introduced to a surly young north German, whom he predicted would 'make a noise in the musical world.' Even Mozart could hardly have guessed the volume of the noise: the youth's name was Ludwig van Beethoven.

Mozart and Constanze arrived in Prague at the end of the summer to prepare for *Don Giovanni*. For a time they stayed at an inn in the centre of the city. It is related that da Ponte stayed at the opposite inn and that they discussed the work in shouted conversations over the heads of passers-by. In fact, most of the later stages of composition were carried out in the Duschek family's villa just outside the city. Other well-known stories tell of Mozart's own Don Giovanni-like behaviour towards the

*Leopold
Mozart's
tombstone*

three female singers and of the completion of the overture on the eve
of the first performance (it was actually finished two nights before). The
Prague singers were not up to Viennese standards and were slow to learn
their parts. This apparently did not deprive them of their right to
criticise the music—the Giovanni required no less than five versions of
'Là ci darem' before he was satisfied. Meanwhile, Mozart directed a performance of *Figaro* before a pair of royal honeymooners visiting Prague,
despite very reasonable doubts as to its aptness.

Don Giovanni was eventually produced on the 29th of October 1787,
to the enormous delight of the Prague audience. Mozart and Constanze
remained in Prague for only two more weeks—he declined an invitation
to stay longer and write another opera. Soon after their return to Vienna,
Mozart had a pleasant surprise when he was appointed chamber
musician to the court in place of Gluck, who had just died. His duties
hardly seem to have been onerous: probably he had to do little more
than provide dances for court balls. One might have hoped that the
extra annual income of eight hundred gulden would have solved his
pecuniary troubles. It is hard to see why it did not. But the sad fact is
that during the next year Mozart plunged deeper and deeper into debt,
and early in the summer the pitiful and embarrassing sequence of begging letters to a brother freemason, the wealthy merchant Michael
Puchberg, began.

In May 1788 *Don Giovanni* had its first Viennese performance.
Mozart added a number of new arias to suit the singers available in the
capital, but although the work was given fifteen more performances
during the year it was no great success—lighter, less demanding music
was more to the Viennese taste.

The early months of 1788 had seen the composition of only one full-scale work, a piano concerto. But in June a move to new lodgings broke the spell of infertility. On the 27th he wrote to Puchberg: 'During the ten days since I came to live here I have done more work than in two months in my former quarters . . . my rooms are pleasant—comfortable —and—cheap.' A few days before, he had completed a masterly piano trio, while only the previous evening he had put the final touches to an Adagio for strings, a piano sonata and the great E flat Symphony. Before another six weeks had passed he had added to these a violin sonata, a piano trio and the other two parts of the mighty triptych which crowns his orchestral music, the symphonies in G minor and C. One could hardly complain if he were left exhausted by so prodigious a creative outburst, but in fact the early autumn produced two valuable chamber works, a string trio for Puchberg and a final piano trio, besides some more or less frivolous vocal canons.

By this time Mozart's position in Vienna's musical life was declining. Pupils were falling off and after seven years the notoriously fickle Viennese music-lovers were no longer anxious to hear him. In the autumn a useful commission came from Baron van Swieten. As director of van Swieten's concerts, Mozart was asked to satisfy his patron's enthusiastic appetite for Handel by arranging such works as *Messiah* and *Acis and Galatea* for the resources available. To us, with a keener historical sense than Mozart and his contemporaries, the arrangements may seem a travesty of Handel and an unconvincing mixture of styles. But by the canons of his own day Mozart was not guilty of a lapse of taste: to him it could only have seemed that he was bringing up to date, as far as possible, some works which were rather primitively scored.

A view of Prague

With the situation in Vienna virtually stagnant, Mozart must have welcomed the invitation from his pupil Prince Lichnowsky to accompany him to Berlin in spring 1789. Perhaps Mozart felt a bitter touch of nostalgia for the travelling days of his youth as they journeyed, through Prague, to Dresden. The latest piano concerto pleased the Elector of Saxony, who rewarded him with the inevitable snuff-box; and the new string trio, together with arias from *Figaro* and *Don Giovanni* sung by Mozart's old friend Mme. Duschek, entertained a private musical party in the Saxon capital.

In Dresden Mozart was not much impressed by the famous organist Hässler—'he has done no more than commit to memory the harmony and modulations of old Sebastian Bach and is not capable of executing a fugue properly'. Playing himself, Mozart delighted those of his hearers who had expected him to be unfamiliar with the north German organ style. At Leipzig he played at the Thomaskirche, which half a century before had echoed to the improvisations of the great J. S. Bach. The aged cantor, Doles, is reported to have said that his old master must be risen again, and he in turn impressed Mozart with a performance of Bach's motet *Singet dem Herrn*, which like most of Bach's music was almost certainly unfamiliar to Mozart.

Mozart stayed only briefly in Leipzig before going on to Potsdam. He returned after a few days, at Lichnowsky's insistence, to give a public concert there—a wasted journey, for the concert, which included two piano concertos and two of the new symphonies, was financially a failure. The visits to Potsdam and Berlin were more successful. He gave no public concerts as they were discouraged by Friedrich Wilhelm II, but was generously rewarded for playing at court, and the King, himself a keen cellist, commissioned a set of six string quartets and a set of six piano sonatas for his daughter. Possibly Mozart was offered a post at the court, but this seems unlikely, for he surely would have accepted it. He heard *The Seraglio* at the theatre and may have had a brief affair with one of the singers.

He arrived back in Vienna at the beginning of June, after two months' absence. The tour had not been very profitable. At one point he had even had to lend money to Lichnowsky; he could hardly refuse, he wrote to Constanze—one can all too easily imagine why. Within six weeks of his return Mozart was ill and once again in desperate straits. He wrote to Puchberg:

'Great God! I would not wish my worst enemy to be in my present position. And if you, most beloved friend and brother, forsake me, we are altogether lost, *both my unfortunate and blameless self* and my poor sick wife and child. . . . Good God! I am coming to you not with thanks but with fresh entreaties! Instead of paying my debts I am asking for more money! If you really know me, you must sympathise with my anguish in having to do so. I need not tell you once more that

Scene from a production of 'Così fan tutte'

owing to my unfortunate illness I have been prevented from earning anything. But I must mention that in spite of my wretched condition I decided to give subscription concerts at home in order to be able to meet at least my present great and frequent expenses. . . . A fortnight ago I sent round a list for subscribers and so far the only name on it is that of Baron van Swieten !'

Puchberg once more helped to relieve the situation and soon Constanze was packed off for a cure at Baden, a few miles from Vienna. Rumours that his wife was conforming to the free and easy standards pertaining there disquieted Mozart, as his admonitory letters to her show. Meanwhile, he started work on the Prussian commissions and also found time to write the clarinet Quintet for his unscrupulous friend Anton Stadler.

But the autumn's main task was a new opera, *Così fan tutte* (the title is not really translatable—something like '*Women—they're all the same!*' is a near approximation to the original sense). The new work, lighter in style than *Don Giovanni*, was much more to Viennese taste and was far better received. It was first given in January 1790 and had a long run, interrupted for a while by court mourning when Joseph II died.

The success of his opera did not help Mozart to exorcise the grim spectre of ever-increasing debt. He had hopes of better treatment from the new Emperor, but his application for the post of second kapellmeister was rejected. While all Vienna was whistling the tunes of *Così* Mozart was writing more abject and grovelling letters to Puchberg,

Mit gnädigster Erlaubniß
Wird Heute Freytags den 15ten October 1790.
im grosen Stadt-Schauspielhause
Herr Kapellmeister Mozart
ein grosses
musikalisches Konzert
zu seinem Vortheil geben.

Erster Theil.
Eine neue grose Simphonie von Herrn Mozart.
Eine Arie, gesungen von Madame Schick.
Ein Concert auf dem Forte-piano, gespielt von Herrn Kapellmeister Mozart von seiner eigenen Komposition.
Eine Arie, gesungen von Herrn Cecarelli.

Zwenter Theil.
Ein Concert von Herrn Kapellmeister Mozart von seiner eigenen Komposition.
Ein Duett, gesungen von Madame Schick und Herrn Cecarelli.
Eine Phantasie aus dem Stegreife von Herrn Mozart.
Eine Symphonie.

Die Person zahlt in den Logen und Parquet a fl. 45 kr
Auf der Gallerie 24 kr.

Billets sind bey Herrn Mozart, wohnhaft in der Kahlbrechergasse Nro. 167. vom Donnerstag Nachmittags und Freytags Früh bey Herrn Cassier Scheidtweiler und an der Casse zu haben.

Der Anfang ist um Eilf Uhr Vormittags.

Handbill of Mozart's concert in Frankfurt, 15th October, 1790

pitifully begging for help, with assurances of the excellent prospects of speedy repayment—prospects in which Mozart was deceiving himself, if not Puchberg. Constanze's next baby arrived and, like the previous one, departed; the efficacy of Nature's crude method of population control must have been a relief as well as a sadness to the hard-pressed couple, for whom their one surviving child was quite enough of a burden.

Composition proceeded slowly. By the end of summer 1790 the only works of any substance written since *Così* were two of the string quartets for Friedrich Wilhelm II. A few abortive sketches of piano sonata movements show that he was trying to work on the other part of the Prussian commission, but ideas were not coming readily. On his return from Berlin the previous summer he had composed one quartet and one sonata; he failed to complete the rest of the commission and never wrote again for string quartet or solo piano.

The succession of Leopold II meant that there would be coronation festivities in various parts of his extensive empire. Several members of the court's musical establishment—excluding Mozart—were sent to Frankfurt in autumn 1790 for the celebrations there. Mozart decided to go too, to give a concert while the town was full and in festive mood. But his concert clashed with other attractions. As he wrote to Constanze: 'It was a splendid success from the point of view of honour and glory, but a failure as far as money was concerned.' The programme included two piano concertos, one of which has consequently been dubbed the 'Coronation'. He travelled home through Mainz, where he played at court, then through the town of Offenbach (meeting the publisher André) to Mannheim, where he stayed a few days to help with a performance of *Figaro*. His last stop was at Munich, where he played at court before the visiting King of Naples, during whose recent visit to Vienna he had been passed over.

Back in Vienna, life was uneventful—too uneventful. An invitation to London, to compose two operas, had to be refused for some reason; in December Mozart saw Haydn leave for the English capital, and was promised an opportunity to be Salomon's next guest in that wealthy and musical city. Meanwhile, he steeled himself to the task of composing pieces for a mechanical organ, a kind of composition he particularly disliked. But during the next few months he also wrote his autumnal last piano concerto and his last chamber works (a pair of string quintets) as well as many dances and some pieces for glass harmonica.

In spring 1791 Mozart applied for the post of assistant kapellmeister of St. Stephen's Cathedral. There is bitter irony in the fact that just this one of his many applications was successful: first, since the post was unpaid, and second, since it carried the virtual promise of the full kapellmeistership on the death of the then elderly incumbent—who in fact outlived Mozart by two years.

His last summer was a busy one. Constanze, expecting a baby (who was to survive, and eventually to become a professional pianist), was away in Baden for several weeks with their son. Mozart wrote to her almost daily, affectionate letters, full of childlike humour, usually about money matters or their various friends. He often went out to visit her, and struck up a friendship with the local organist, for whom he wrote the motet *Ave verum corpus*. While Constanze was away Mozart spent his spare time with various friends—the Puchbergs, whose kind and frequent invitations to lunch were very welcome, Ignaz Leutgeb, his cheesemonger-cum-hornist friend from Salzburg, and another old acquaintance, Emanuel Schikaneder, with whom he spent what may euphemistically be called some gay evenings.

His working hours were occupied in a different kind of collaboration with Schikaneder. This shrewd man of the theatre—writer, producer, actor and singer—had suggested that they should devise a kind of musical pantomime, *Die Zauberflöte* (*The Magic Flute*), for production at the popular theatre of which he was manager. Initially, Mozart was not keen on the plan, but as the work took shape his enthusiasm grew. Working at it steadily in a summer-house near the theatre, where Schikaneder could keep an eye on him, the opera was virtually completed in July.

During that month another commission arrived. A mysterious stranger clad in grey called one day to ask Mozart to compose a Requiem,

Count Walsegg

Emanuel Schikaneder

under conditions of absolute secrecy. The stranger was in fact an emissary of a Viennese nobleman, Count Walsegg, who wished to pass the work off as his own. But Mozart knew nothing of this. Being ill and depressed as well as superstitious, he read sinister meanings into the event and set to work with his mind full of dark foreboding.

While work was in progress on the Requiem, Mozart received yet another commission. This time it was from Prague. Leopold II was to be crowned King of Bohemia in the autumn and a festive opera was required. A suitable subject had to be found quickly, so an old libretto by Metastasio, *La clemenza di Tito*, was chosen, and revised by Caterino Mazzolà for the occasion. It was still very unsatisfactory, but Mozart was in no position to decline two hundred ducats, and in any case Prague held happy memories as the scene of former successes. So at the end of August Mozart and Constanze set off, taking Mozart's pupil Süssmayr to give a hand with the routine work on the recitatives. The whole opera was ready in two-and-a-half weeks and had its first performance on the 6th of September. It is hardly surprising that it was no great success. Failing in health and depressed in spirit, Mozart returned to Vienna, for the last time.

He put the final touches to *The Magic Flute* on the 28th of September and the next day completed his last instrumental work, the clarinet Concerto. On the 30th *Titus* had its last performance (a successful one) in Prague while *The Magic Flute* had its first in Vienna. At first this strange work, with its masonic symbolism and its curious mixture of the sublime and the ridiculous, puzzled the middle-class audiences at Schikaneder's theatre. But it quickly became very popular, and had no less than twenty-four performances in October. Constanze's eldest sister, Josefa, sang the Queen of Night's part while Schikaneder himself played Papageno. Mozart wrote to Constanze, again away in Baden, that Salieri was present at one performance and 'there was not a single number that did not call forth from him a bravo! or bello!'.

The rest of the story is all too simple. When Constanze came home from Baden she found Mozart weak and gloomy, but feverishly at work on the Requiem. Ideas that he was writing his own Requiem, and that he had poisoned himself, took hold of him. During November he had a more lucid spell and was able to throw off such notions; he was even well enough to compose a masonic cantata and to direct a performance of it in public.

But that was his last public appearance. A few days later he took to his bed, in rapidly worsening condition. Doctors and apothecaries could do little for him. His wife and her youngest sister, Sophie, nursed him with devotion. He still worked on the Requiem, discussing it with Süssmayr; sometimes a few friends would gather to sing over passages from it. On the 3rd of December, Sophie relates, he was rather better, and talking of getting up. But when she called the next day she found Constanze distraught and Mozart facing death. With difficulty she persuaded a priest to come to administer the final rites, and with still more difficulty she found the doctor, who was at the theatre and would come only when the play was finished. When he arrived he ordered cold poultices to be placed on Mozart's burning head, which had the effect of making him unconscious. At midnight Mozart turned on his side, as if to sleep. Just under one hour later, on the 5th of December, he died.

The cause of his death has not been definitely established. Uraemia, rheumatic fever, consumption, goitre, dropsy, Bright's disease, mercury poisoning, miliary fever and brain inflammation have all been among the posthumous diagnoses. Rumours that he was poisoned by Salieri need not be taken too seriously—and in any case, what had the thriving chief court composer to gain from poisoning so ineffective a rival? In making funeral arrangements Constanze consulted Baron van Swieten, who merely told her of the cheapest method. So on the 6th of December Mozart was buried, along with several others, in a pauper's grave at St. Mark's, just outside the city. The actual position of his grave remains unknown. Van Swieten, Süssmayr, Salieri, at least two Viennese musicians and probably Mozart's two brothers-in-law were present at the funeral. The story of a severe storm, and the mourners' turning back, is untrue: it was in fact a mild, damp day, and there is no evidence about who was present at the actual interment.

It only remains to say what happened to Constanze. She found herself deeply in debt on her husband's death. In a petition to the Emperor she

The last page of Mozart's autograph score of the Requiem (the two bars ringed in pencil are believed to be by Josef Eybler; Süssmayr did not use them in the final version)

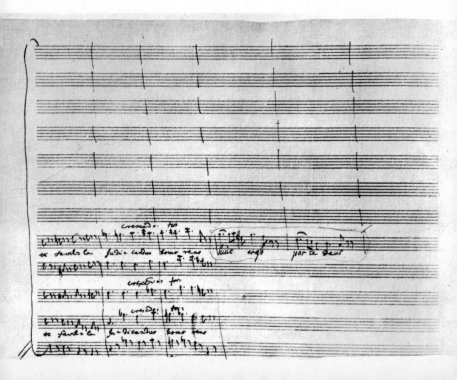

described her situation, mentioning incidentally two offers of regular income to Mozart, from Holland and Hungary, which had come too late to be of use (no doubt they would have gone the way of all such previous plans had they come sooner). The Emperor advised her to arrange a concert, which he himself patronised with sufficient generosity to put her position to rights. Some years later she married Georg Nikolaus von Nissen, who wrote a biography of Mozart and helped her with the monumental task of sorting and selling his manuscripts. And so ends the tale of a life which in worldly terms may have been a failure but in terms of artistic achievement was one of the greatest of all success stories.

CONVENIT IGITUR---IN GESTU NEC
VENUSTATEM CONSPICUAM, NEC TUR-
DINEM ESSE, NE AUT HISTRIONES,
AUT OPERARII VIDEAMUR ESSE.

G. Eichler delin.

Jac. Andr. Fridrich Sc. A.V.

Frontispiece of Leopold Mozart's 'Violin School' (1756)

The Growth of Mozart's Style

No artist can exist in isolation. Mozart certainly never wished to do so. Perhaps more than any other great composer, he was profoundly affected by contacts with his contemporaries, and in the following pages we shall see how these contacts played a crucial role in the growth of his style.

First it may be useful to sketch in the musical background of Mozart's childhood. Among his instruction books were no doubt Leopold's *Violin School* and C. P. E. Bach's *Essay on the True Art of Keyboard Playing* (1753). The first pieces he played were from the manuscript books copied by Leopold in 1759 and 1762, mainly of short dance movements by the most progressive composers of Leopold's generation and the preceding one, many of them north Germans, like Telemann, C. P. E. Bach and Hasse, with a characteristic technical solidity and stylistic clarity. He probably also used printed collections of Italian keyboard music, including pieces by such men as Galuppi, Pescetti and Rutini—fluent, facile composers with a light, easy-going and up-to-date melodic style. The music he heard was by local composers—Eberlin, Michael Haydn, Adlgasser and Leopold himself—and perhaps the leading Viennese figures, among them Wagenseil, Gassmann and Gluck.

When Mozart made his first long journey from Salzburg, as a boy of eight, he found new worlds of music opening before him. The musical stimuli he encountered on these travels were to affect him profoundly. In Paris, where there was perpetual conflict in the operatic sphere between native French and imported Italian elements, the important field of salon music was dominated by a group of German composers—Schobert, Eckard, Honauer, Raupach and others. French music itself had little effect on Mozart; when Leopold wrote 'The whole of French music isn't worth a fig,' he was merely repeating what was almost regarded as axiomatic by Germans, Italians and Englishmen alike, and by not a few Frenchmen.

Of the German Parisians, Schobert was indisputably the leader, and a most accomplished composer. Though his music was designed to satisfy the appetites of the fashionable Parisian music-lovers, it did more than that. Schobert was profoundly affected by the wave of near-Romantic seriousness which swept across all European artistic activities in the early 1760s, and his music has an energetic, impassioned quality which must have seemed new and exciting to the boy, so far brought up along rather conservative lines. The form used most by Schobert and his colleagues was the accompanied sonata. (A reminder may be useful at this point: in the accompanied sonata the keyboard was the principal instrument and the violinist did the accompanying.) This musically rather unsatisfactory form—it eventually developed into the genuine violin-piano duo and the piano trio—was well suited to social conditions of the time and was very popular with the music-buying public. Apart from childish miniatures, it is the first form which Mozart attempted, when he wrote four sonatas in Paris [6-9]* and six in London [10-15].

It is clear from these sonatas how much Schobert had impressed him. They are not on Schobert's emotional scale—that would be impossible for a child—nor are they as virtuoso in style. By the standards of the time they are no more than ordinary music, with a certain pale charm, and a good deal too much 'Alberti bass'. But one movement, the Adagio of K.7, certainly reflects his new contact with music of a more emotional character. He also learnt from Schobert in a more direct way. The prototype for the texture of the last movement of Mozart's first sonata is clearly the opening of one Schobert sonata, while the actual material is closely related to another:

*Köchel numbers are given in square brackets where they are necessary for identification. On account of their greater familiarity, the numbers given, with a few unavoidable exceptions, are those from Köchel's earlier editions rather than the Einstein revision.

Johann Christian Bach (oil painting by Gainsborough)

A theme in one of the sonatas written in London, K.12, is just as plainly derived from a sonata by Eckard.

The journey to London brought Mozart into contact with two important figures, C. F. Abel and J. C. Bach. Abel's influence on Mozart is not of special significance. Mozart copied out one of his symphonies, a regular and well-proportioned work, to serve as an example of the new symphonic form which was now beginning to interest him, and later he occasionally recalled in his music phrases from works by Abel which he must have heard in London. J. C. Bach's role was much more crucial. This extremely gifted composer, trained by his father and his half-brother C. P. E. Bach, had spent some years in Italy between his youth in Germany and his maturity in London; there he had fertilised his sound German technique with Italianate grace, vivacity and melodic fluency. Naturally the young Mozart was deeply impressed by this supreme master of the galant style.

It is easy to see J. C. Bach's influence in the melodic shapes and the actual forms of Mozart's London sonatas, and in a whole host of features in the early symphonies—the sharp alternations of *forte* and *piano*, the frequent repetitions of phrases, the clear separation of sections by formal cadences, the 'singing' quality of many of the themes, the dashing finales, often in 'hunting' style and in rondo form, and the 'semi–sonata form' first movements (with no recapitulation of the first subject in the home key). Most of these are basically Italian characteristics, but very up-to-date ones which Mozart had not met before—or, if he had met them, he had not heard them used with such significance or technical aplomb.

A phrase from a J. C. Bach piano concerto occurs in Mozart's third authentic symphony, written just after the visit to London:

More than twenty years later it reappears in *Figaro*, in J. C. Bach's original key:

This may serve to illustrate that Mozart never entirely forgot J. C. Bach's music. In several works he made direct quotations: examples are the piano Rondo, K.485, based on a theme from a popular Bach quintet, and the Andante of the piano Concerto in A [414], which opens with a theme from a Bach symphony and seems like an elegy on hearing of Bach's death (an event Mozart lamented as 'a loss to the musical world'). During his 1778 visit to Paris Mozart had a letter from Leopold urging him to write in Bach's 'natural, flowing and easy style', pointing out that he would not be lowering himself by composing such potentially popular music as long as it bore the hall-mark of sound technique. He did not ignore the advice. The piano sonatas he wrote that summer—and particularly the one in B flat [333], probably written just after the receipt of Leopold's letter—show that he was making a conscious attempt to copy J. C. Bach's popular and elegant style. Among other movements indebted to Bach are the *menuet en rondeau* finales in such works as the bassoon Concerto [191] and the flute Concerto in G [313].

Another work in which J. C. Bach's influence appears, somewhat unexpectedly, is the 'little' G minor Symphony, No. 25 [183]. Bach's main field of activity was light, graceful music, but he occasionally permitted himself a more serious work; one such is his G minor Symphony, op. 6 no. 6. Mozart, in his 25th Symphony, may have leant to a slight extent on Haydn's minor-key symphonies (such as nos. 39 and 44) or those by Vanhal, but in fact the work is more closely related to Bach's. Apart from a strong general similarity in mood and atmosphere, there are some manifest resemblances—between the opening descending fourths, and more particularly between the two composers' treatment of the same rhythmic figure, ♩♫ , which in each case reappears in the last movement.

Altogether, J. C. Bach emerges as a key figure in Mozart's development. The fact that his influence was so considerable derives ultimately from a special affinity of spirit between the two men, related, perhaps, to the happy blend of northern and southern elements in their music.

In Mozart's childhood environment, Italian music (and particularly opera) was regarded as the most cultured and sophisticated, even the highest, form of musical art. Italy, the birthplace of all the principal musical forms and ideas over the previous two centuries, was to Mozart and his German contemporaries the musical country *par excellence*. Though Mozart was proud of being German, it was always with the slightly self-conscious pride of one who instinctively felt that Germans were, on the whole, a trifle less inherently musical than Italians.

During his first visit to Italy, Mozart quickly picked up the current Italian manner. It is easy to see, by comparing the symphonies he wrote there in 1770 with those written earlier in Vienna, how he adopted the style of such composers as Sacchini, Anfossi and Piccini. The symphonies K.81 and 84 show strong Italian characteristics—their three-movement form, their brevity, their conventional orchestral figuration, their lightness and brilliance of style with emphasis on melodic ideas rather than development. Another aspect of Italian influence is seen in the contrapuntal studies Mozart undertook in Bologna under Padre Martini. Although a contrapuntal style was used universally for church music,

Nicola Piccini (engraving after Robineau)

the kind of counterpoint taught by Martini, stemming from the poly-phonic Renaissance style which had reached its peak two hundred years earlier in the music of Palestrina and his contemporaries, was particularly Italianate in its clarity and smoothness.

But Mozart was at his most obviously Italian in his operas. From *Mitridate*, written at Milan in 1770, to *La clemenza di Tito*, composed in 1791, Mozart's musical language was basically the same as that of his Italian contemporaries when he was setting Italian words. The phrase-lengths, the melodic contours and the cadences were as dependent on the natural rhythms and vowel-sounds of the Italian tongue when set by Mozart as when set by any other composer. Moreover, since Italian composers and Italian music played so dominant a role in eighteenth-century European musical life, phrases which owed their origins to

Italian speech rhythms permeated the ordinary musical language of the time. The standard feminine cadences are an obvious example.

Apart from such generalised Italian influence it is possible to find in Mozart's music direct reminiscences of particular Italian composers, just like those of J. C. Bach quoted above. It must be emphasised at this point that the quotation of a theme from some other composer's music does not in itself mean that Mozart was influenced by that composer. It happens, however, to be a particularly convenient way of demonstrating that the composer's music had some impact, conscious or (more likely) subconscious, on Mozart's mind and his musical personality. Influence, of course, extends far beyond the reproduction of themes, but its larger-scale manifestations cannot readily be shown without printing long stretches of music in full score.

At one time or another Mozart quoted from virtually every leading Italian composer of his day. He was particularly indebted to Pasquale Anfossi. Anfossi's setting of *La finta giardiniera* had been highly successful all over Europe and Mozart did not hesitate to model his own setting on it. He later came into contact with Anfossi's music in Paris and Vienna: his ballet *Les petits riens*, written in Paris for insertion in operas by Piccini and Anfossi, recalls a phrase from the latter's overture to *La vera costanza*:

Another composer from whom Mozart quoted is Sacchini. A theme from the overture to one of his most popular operas, *Il Cid*, appears in *The Seraglio*:

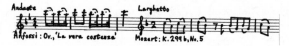

The fandango from *Figaro*, though partly borrowed from Gluck's *Don Juan* ballet, finds another pre-echo in a ballet from the French version of *Il Cid*. As Dent has shown, Sarti and Paisiello also provided Mozart with important 'springboards' for items in *Figaro*. In *Don Giovanni*, there is a possible link between the minuet in the Act I finale and a movement from Salieri's *Armida*, while the villagers' chorus clearly derives from a song in Piccini's *Vittorina*:

83

Piccini may also have provided the initial idea behind the main theme of *The Magic Flute* overture, in a quartet from his opera *Il Barone di Torreforte*. But the more obvious source here is a piano sonata by Clementi, who recorded in the edition he later published that he had played the work before the Austrian Emperor in Mozart's presence, no doubt at their encounter in 1781.

In Mozart's instrumental music generally, Italian elements are outweighed by German or Austrian ones. His first significant contact with Viennese composers came during his visit to the capital in 1767. There are marked differences in style between the earlier symphonies and the group dating from these months, whose Viennese origins are seen in their richer orchestration, their full sonata form and their inclusion of minuets. The emphasis Mozart gave to his minuets in several succeeding symphonies, even occasionally using imitative treatment (as in K.73 and 110), suggests the specific influence of the most important member of the Viennese school, Joseph Haydn.

It was not until 1773, however, that Mozart really began to perceive the significance of Haydn's music. In 1771-2 Haydn had published two sets of string quartets, op. 17 and op. 20: with a Germanic seriousness of approach, he had added weight and strength to the form by laying greater emphasis on the development of themes and by increasing the interest of the second violin and viola parts. The six quartets Mozart wrote during his visit to Vienna in 1773 are clearly an attempt to emulate the principal Viennese quartet composer. His familiarity with these Haydn works (and with the earlier op. 9 set) is betrayed by several thematic resemblances. Still more significant are Mozart's use of fugal finales (in K.168 and 173) along the lines of Haydn's op. 20 nos. 2, 3 and 6, the imitation of Haydn's slow movement cantilena style in three of the Mozart quartets and the increasing complexity of Mozart's minuets.

Mozart did not return to the string quartet for another ten years, when he started on the set of six to be dedicated to Haydn. In 1781 Haydn's op. 33 set had appeared, described by the composer as 'written in a new and special manner', the novelty lying in the treatment of thematic development and the tendency towards a still more equal relationship between the instruments. The Mozart set shows a definite debt to op. 33, in the way important material is often given to the inner parts and in the generally concentrated nature of the style (there is even one mono-thematic movement, the finale of K.464)—though it is as well to remember that Mozart, with a very strong instinctive sense of form and tremendous melodic fertility, always had a different attitude from Haydn to thematic material and its treatment. Again, one can demonstrate Mozart's familiarity with the Haydn quartets by their echoes, no doubt subconscious, in his own: Mozart's 6/8 variation finale in K.421 is indebted to Haydn's in no. 5, while the openings of the minuets in the two E flat quartets (K.428 and no. 2) are markedly alike.

The genial Michael Haydn is almost as significant a figure in Mozart's

JOSEPH HAYDN.

development as his more purposeful elder brother. Mozart heard much of Michael Haydn's church music in his early years and had a firm respect and admiration for it, copying out several of his sacred works and modelling his own *Te Deum* [141] exactly on one of Michael's. It would be wrong, though, to suggest that Michael Haydn was the only influence here: others of importance are Eberlin (a former Salzburg organist), the Viennese composer Gassmann, and particularly Hasse, a thoroughly Italianised and therefore fashionable German composer who was a leading representative of the smooth, sensuous style of Neapolitan church music. In the instrumental field, Mozart's divertimentos and serenades follow the established Austrian pattern, and here he learnt much from Michael Haydn, who was near at hand and one of the form's leading exponents. Probably it was Michael's example that stimulated him, in 1773, to try the rather unusual string quintet form.

Mozart's mature symphonies also show his influence. In the *Linz* Symphony, no. 36 [425], the rather sinister F minor episode in the slow movement (bar 45 f.) was clearly suggested by a similar passage in a Michael Haydn Symphony in G—that very symphony which Mozart included, with his own slow introduction [444], in the concert where the *Linz* was first performed. The seeds of the principal theme in the first movement of no. 39 in E flat [543] can be seen in an E flat symphony by Michael Haydn, and the slow movements—both in the unusual key of A flat and in 2/4 time—also have points of resemblance. Mozart was in Salzburg when Michael Haydn was finishing this symphony, in summer 1783, and we may be sure that he knew it.

The contrapuntal finale of the *Jupiter* Symphony, no. 41 [551], is another movement where Mozart followed Michael Haydn. Mozart's use of fugal processes has often been traced back to his enthusiasm for the contrapuntal music of J. S. Bach and Handel. It is easy to exaggerate this enthusiasm. Mozart was admittedly affected by the general wave of interest in baroque music, and Bach's music in particular, which traversed musical Europe in the 1780s. His contact with works by Bach and Handel at Baron van Swieten's house in 1782 set him thinking about contrapuntal forms, and he sent home for fugues by them and Eberlin —later countermanding the request for Eberlin's, which he realised were unworthy of such company. Constanze, to whom he was then engaged, was particularly fond of fugues, which no doubt spurred his interest. To this period belong a number of fugues for piano and piano duet (mostly unfinished, like practically all the music he wrote for Constanze), the Fantasia and Fugue in C [394], the incomplete Suite in C [399] (which is a deliberate attempt to imitate the style of a baroque keyboard suite), a violin Sonata [402] with an unfinished fugal finale, and several transcriptions of fugues and other movements by Bach. A climax came in the two-piano Fugue in C minor [426] and, perhaps, in the fugal writing of the unfinished C minor Mass [427]. But this last can also serve as a reminder that Mozart had never ceased to be a contra-

Michael Haydn

puntal composer when he was writing for the church; counterpoint was simply a part of the normal language of church music and Mozart was not returning to it in response to any particular stimulus.

Most of these works can be seen either as attempts to please Constanze or as experiments in a musical language which had always interested Mozart but which he had not much cultivated lately. They all lie well off the main stream of his musical development: he did not follow them up and they had no appreciable effect upon the major items of his output in the following years. It is true that many works from about 1786 onwards show a quickening interest in the occasional use of contrapuntal processes, but this in any case is far from uncommon as a means of concentration and intensification of thought among composers reaching maturity—Beethoven is an obvious example. To talk of Mozart's contact with Bach's music as causing 'a revolution and a crisis in his creative activity', as Einstein does in his excellent book, is to read into this episode a disproportionate significance. Mozart admired Bach's music, as a discerning critic was bound to do, but in the historical circumstances it is impossible that he could have done so with the fervour and intensity with which we regard it today, and to impute such ideas to him is romantically wishful thinking.

It was also during this period that Mozart wrote the Quartet in G [387]. His use of fugal processes here is especially significant. By absorbing them into a sonata-form type of framework, as he did in the finale of this quartet, he gave them a place within the scope of a valid expressive medium of his time. The usage of fugue here is distinct from that in two of the 1773 quartets mentioned above, where the finales, fugues pure and simple, are almost archaistic in style. Possibly Mozart's interest in fugue was fired by contact with baroque music at van Swieten's concerts: but it would be foolish to suppose that it was Bach's or Handel's influence which induced him to achieve a fusion between fugue and sonata form.

In any case, Mozart was not the only one to attempt this kind of fusion. A senior composer of the Mannheim school, Franz Xaver Richter, had shown a fondness for fugal finales, and in one symphony at least had written a binary form finale with a fugal beginning to each half of the movement but a clearly marked non-fugal second subject. Richter, too, was only one of several composers who considered the possibilities of fugue within the framework of a more progressive form. Others include two important Viennese figures, Monn and Dittersdorf, and a third was Michael Haydn—which brings us back to the point of departure for this brief discussion on Mozart's use of fugue. Five of Michael Haydn's forty-six known symphonies have 'fugato' finales, and four of these pre-date the *Jupiter*. Mozart was certainly acquainted with some of them; he even copied out part of one fugal finale, beginning with a phrase not unlike the *Jupiter* fugue subject:

The others, two of them in C major like the *Jupiter*, include phrases very similar to the simple contrapuntal tags which Mozart used. It certainly appears that Michael Haydn, working in a tradition stemming from the period when composers like Richter and Monn included contrapuntal movements in their symphonies, has strong claims for providing the stimulus behind the *Jupiter* finale.

The Mannheim school, mentioned above in passing, represents another important influence on Mozart. We saw earlier how impressed he was by the high standard of the Mannheim orchestra and by the musical atmosphere in the Palatine capital. A distinctive style had evolved at Mannheim, partly based on the orchestral techniques which had been developed there. Probably the Mannheim school made no great innovations, but they adopted and made their own a number of

A view of the electoral court at Mannheim

musical mannerisms (Leopold once wrote punningly about the 'mannered Mannheimers'). Their crescendo, which according to one critic could make listeners rise gradually from their seats in excitement, was particularly famous; previously, alternating loud and soft sections had been the general rule in orchestral music. Use of the string tremolando was another favourite Mannheim effect, as were abrupt dynamic alternations, dashing violin scales ('Mannheim rockets') and an extremely expressive style of writing in slow movements (including the 'Mannheim sigh').

Mozart had of course met the Mannheim style during his musical upbringing. There are occasional signs of it in his early works, such as the typical Mannheim crescendo in the overture to *Il rè pastore*, of 1775. But on his visit to Mannheim in 1777 he quickly responded to the music he heard there. The first work he wrote in the city was the piano Sonata in C [309]; its Andante is full of dynamic shading and expressive sighs, and Leopold, after seeing the first two movements, wrote: 'one can see from its style that you composed it in Mannheim.'

The Mannheim manner is not particularly evident in the two flute concertos composed there—at the request of the amateur who commissioned them, they were written in a simple style. It is naturally in Mozart's symphonic music that signs of it are mostly to be found. The

Paris Symphony [297], his next major orchestral work, is one example. There are certainly concessions here to the Parisian taste, such as the opening *coup d'archet*, the clarity of the formal outlines and the general lightness and brilliance of style. But between Mannheim and Paris there was musically speaking no great distance; in fact, the Mannheim symphonists provided much of the Parisian repertory. It was largely through his contact with the Mannheim composers that Mozart was able to speak the Parisian symphonic language with such fluency and élan.

A favourite form at Mannheim was the sinfonia concertante, or multiple concerto, where the virtuosos in the orchestra could shine in solo parts. It is not surprising that Mozart's Sinfonia Concertante for violin and viola [364], written soon after his return to Salzburg, has strong leanings to the Mannheim style (so has the wind Sinfonia Concertante [297b], whether authentic or not). There is no need to look beyond the opening ritornello of K.364 to see such characteristic features as long, tense crescendos, sharply alternating loud and soft passages, and tuttis with the main melodic line in the bass below violin tremolandos. Mozart plainly had in mind the works for the same combination by Carl Stamitz, a leading Mannheim composer and son of Johann Stamitz, the school's founder. Written at much the same time were the 32nd Symphony [318] and the *Posthorn* Serenade [320], which also embody Mannheim crescendos and other features of the style.

Gluck, though incomparably the greatest dramatic composer of the 1760s and 70s, had a limited influence on Mozart; the two had radically different operatic outlooks. Mozart admired Gluck, but learnt from him only in the treatment of accompanied recitative (especially from Eurydice's death scene in *Orfeo*) and in certain features of *The Magic Flute* and *Idomeneo*—though in the latter he is more Piccinist than Gluckist.

C. P. E. Bach was another major figure whose influence on Mozart was very limited. The lack of polish and formal discipline characteristic of his music was entirely alien to Mozart, and the only works in which he imitated C. P. E. Bach's style were short keyboard pieces, such as the Fantasias in C minor and D minor [396 and 397] (written at the time of his contact with C. P. E. Bach's music at van Swieten's house), the Fantasia in C minor [475] and the two Rondos [485 and 511], of which the second is at times almost like a parody of C. P. E. Bach's highly chromatic expressive style, besides being in one of his favourite forms.

The remaining influences on Mozart's style can be summarised more briefly. Mozart himself has given us some helpful information in his letters. For example, we know that the six piano and violin sonatas written at Mannheim and Paris were modelled on a set by Joseph Schuster, and it is easy to guess that Georg Benda's duodramas *Ariadne* and *Medea*, which Mozart admired, were the main influence behind his music to *König Thamos*.

Christoph
Willibald von Gluck

It may have been Hiller, a popular composer of Singspiel (German light opera) whose example induced Mozart to write a vaudeville finale in *The Seraglio*, though Gluck's *Orfeo* is an equally likely source for the idea. Dittersdorf, one of Mozart's most gifted German contemporaries, was also esteemed for his Singspiels, but he had little influence on Mozart in this or indeed any other field. It has been suggested that a Dittersdorf concerto, dating from 1773, may have affected the form of Mozart's first piano Concerto [175], written the same year: whether or not this is so, J. C. Bach was undoubtedly the primary influence on Mozart's concerto form—and it is fitting that this section should conclude with a further mention of J. C. Bach, who was by far the most significant figure in Mozart's development as a composer.

Looking back over the foregoing pages, one might be inclined to wonder why Mozart, alone among great composers, went through this elaborate process of moulding his own musical language from those of other men. The basic reason is that, due to his unique precocity, he had opportunities to encounter a wide variety of musical styles during the impressionable years of his youth, and he naturally reacted in the un-inhibited manner of a young person of exceptional sensitivity. It is important to understand that he did not simply switch from one kind of idiom to another as he realised the attractions and potentialities of each one in turn. Rather, he absorbed into his musical personality elements from outside, with the result that by the time he reached musical maturity he had, by continual application—largely at a subconscious level—of the processes of sorting, criticism and evaluation, culminating in rejection or assimilation, forged for himself a musical language which was at the same time individual and universal.

Organ at St. Cajetan's Chapel, Salzburg

The Church Music and Songs

Mozart is not primarily remembered for his church music or his songs. In either medium it is easy to name other composers whose contributions are very reasonably rated higher. With the possible exception of two works, both incomplete, he never made the kind of concentrated effort to excel here as he did in such spheres as opera, orchestral music or chamber music. Moreover, as regards church music and song, there are special religious and aesthetic difficulties which impede our artistic communication with Mozart's era.

In the field of church music, we can listen happily to the spacious serenity of the Renaissance composers, the exuberant grandeur of the baroque masters and the morbid extravagances of the Romantics; and all are acceptable as satisfying to some part of our religious natures. But the worldly religious attitudes of Mozart's time have little in common with those we like to think of as typical of the mid-twentieth century. They are reflected as much in the florid rococo church architecture to be seen in Austria and Southern Germany as in the gay and frankly operatic nature of Catholic sacred music of the time. The secular passions could be moved in the opera house by means of expressive arias and elaborate ornamentation; to Mozart and his contemporaries there was nothing incongruous about applying the same means to the very proper purpose of moving the religious passions in church. There was no question, as far as Mozart was concerned, of changing his language when moving from secular to sacred music—though naturally traditions, and differences in the available resources, affected his ecclesiastical style.

Mozart's church music comprises, altogether, sixteen masses, one Requiem mass, seven other full-scale works such as vespers and litanies, and more than thirty shorter works—offertories, motets and the like, or single mass movements. All but some half-dozen of these are entirely unknown even to the keen Mozartean, and the vast majority, dating from his early years, are likely to remain so.

Most of the sacred works of Mozart's youth were written for immediate use in Salzburg Cathedral. In church music, above all, it was the composer's job to conform to current usage; that is why Mozart simply modelled his early sacred pieces on those of his senior colleagues at Salzburg. A mass could vary considerably in length, from well over an hour for a Missa solemnis to less than half an hour for a Missa brevis. The long mass was designed for more formal occasions and the music was usually fairly elaborate, with the long Gloria and Credo texts divided up to form several movements in contrasting styles. In the short mass each of these sections was set as a single movement, often with a few changes in tempo and metre. The general musical style was melodic rather than contrapuntal. Although it was traditional to conclude the Gloria with a fugue to the words 'Cum sancto spiritu' and the Credo with one to 'Et vitam venturi', the choruses otherwise depended primarily on block writing, with only the simplest use of imitation.

From the time Colloredo succeeded to the Salzburg archbishopric the short mass predominated, for he was a liberal churchman and did not like the more ceremonial form. Mozart wrote to Padre Martini in 1776:

'Our church music is very different from that of Italy, since a mass with the whole Kyrie, the Gloria, the Credo, the Epistle Sonata, the Offertory or Motet, the Sanctus and the Agnus Dei must not last longer than three-quarters of an hour. This applies even to the most solemn mass said by the Archbishop himself. So you see that a special study is required for this kind of composition.'

(During the reading of the Epistle it was normal for a single-movement sonata to be played. Mozart wrote seventeen such pieces, sometimes called Sonate da chiesa or Church Sonatas, mostly for strings and organ —shapely and often high-spirited miniatures.) There are a few masses of the longer type, written before Colloredo's time, of which the one in C minor [139] is by no means an inconsiderable work. But those composed between 1774 and the time he left Salzburg are mostly short. Two dating from 1774 [192 and 194] are miniatures indeed: designed for use on ordinary Sundays, they have accompaniments only for violins and continuo (that is, bass strings and organ), and the words are declaimed with a haste which is only just decent. A particular point of interest is the construction of the Credo of K.194. The liturgical phrase:

St. Peter's Church and Monastery, Salzburg

—famous from its later context in the *Jupiter* Symphony—appears at the opening of the movement and recurs many times, often as a kind of re-affirmation of the words 'Credo, credo', but later to different parts of the text. It even provides the fugue subject for 'Et vitam venturi'.

Another dramatic use of the word 'Credo', this time to a staccato two-note figure, occurs in K.257, which is consequently sometimes called the *Credo* Mass. Two of the six masses written between 1775 and the Paris period are on a larger scale, but much the finest of the Salzburg ones is the first of the pair written after his return, the *Coronation* Mass [317], so called because it was probably written for a ceremonial crowning of the virgin's image.

It is scored for oboes, horns, trumpets, timpani and strings, with three trombones doubling the lower voices of the chorus. The Kyrie is in three sections—a short choral introduction, a lyrical Andante, in dialogue for the soprano and tenor soloists, and a slightly extended and elaborated return of the first part. The Gloria, a triple-time Allegro divided between soloists and chorus, has all the momentum and verve of an Italian symphony, with excursions into the minor at the words 'Qui tollis'. Rushing violin semiquavers give the Credo the usual sense of vigorous affirmation; they are maintained almost continuously except for the Et incarnatus section, where the bustle is suddenly interrupted and the mystery of the words conveyed by the poetic entry of the quartet of soloists, in an Adagio starting in F minor. A solemn Sanctus

95

and a lively Osanna, both short, precede the Benedictus, an Allegretto for the soloists with a gentle sweetness which Mozart often reserved for this section. The most deeply felt movement is the Agnus Dei, starting as a soprano solo with a melody looking ahead to 'Dove sono' in *Figaro*. At 'Dona nobis pacem' the chorus enter with music already heard in the Kyrie; then the tempo speeds up to provide a cheerful if slightly perfunctory ending. This attractive work may serve as a typical example of Mozart's Salzburg church music in its general spirit and outlook as well as in its techniques and treatment.

Before moving on to Mozart's last and greatest masses it will be as well to glance back at the various other sacred works he produced. Among the most important are the four litanies. The text of the two Lorettine litanies [109 and 195] consists largely of supplication to the Virgin, and Mozart put into these works a good deal of appropriately intimate, gentle music of a pleading nature—some of which, one need not hesitate to admit, could serve as well for an operatic lover. The other two [125 and 243] are to the more severe Eucharistic litany text: they include forceful fugues to the words 'Pignus futurae gloriae', that in K.243 being particularly fine, while the Tremendum from the same work has a sinister, dramatic quality which almost suggests Verdi. Two vespers [321 and 339], conceived rather as series of movements than as entities, are not of great importance, but the second cannot be passed over without a mention of one of Mozart's most serenely beautiful melodies, its Laudate Dominum.

Of the shorter works, the best known is the motet *Exsultate, jubilate* [165] for soprano and orchestra, written for the castrato Rauzzini; it is in three movements and is practically a concerto for voice and orchestra. The brilliant concluding Alleluia is deservedly popular. A work Mozart himself took particularly seriously is the offertory *Misericordias Domini* [222] (modelled on an Eberlin *Benedicite*), which he composed at Munich to impress the Elector. He thought well enough of it to send a copy to Padre Martini for criticism, knowing that the venerable theorist would approve its elaborately contrapuntal style. On the same grounds it may seem more like 'real church music' to us than a simple homophonic piece like the short Graduale *Sancta Maria* [273], probably designed as a prayer for divine aid on the journey to Paris, whose personal expressiveness and sincerity are patent. But outstanding among the shorter works is the D minor *Kyrie* [341], a passionate movement, rich in harmony and orchestration—if it was designed to open a mass, we can only regret that Mozart never completed what would surely have been a splendid work.

In fact, Mozart was not to complete another mass. His next attempt was the C minor [427], written to fulfil a vow that he would perform a new mass at Salzburg when he first took Constanze there as his wife. Salzburg tradition has it that K.427 was in fact given there on that occasion, in 1783, but it is highly doubtful since the work was never finished. What remains has aptly been described as a 'noble torso'.

Mozart completed the Kyrie, the Gloria, only two short sections of the Credo, most of the Sanctus and the Benedictus. The profound solemnity of the opening Kyrie suggests a deepening in his religious outlook since the Salzburg days. No less fine are the Qui tollis, a grave movement with eight-part choral writing, often quite chromatic, against a persistent dotted rhythm in the violins, or the blazing C major splendours of the Gloria and the Cum sancto spiritu. Another feature of great interest is the neo-baroque manner Mozart occasionally employs —at the opening of the Domine Deus, for example:

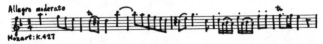

To us, there is apt to seem some incongruity in the conjunction of these elements and the soprano solos (designed for Constanze) of extreme floridity. The Christe eleison and especially the famous Et incarnatus combine virtuoso writing with a considerable degree of expressive intensity, but in the Laudamus te and elsewhere one cannot help feeling that the virtuosity is a little empty and that the work as a whole suffers.

Mozart did not return to church music until his last months, when he wrote the short but entirely perfect funeral motet *Ave verum corpus* [618] and the Requiem [626]. The Requiem was not, of course, completed by Mozart. We can never know exactly how much of it he wrote himself and how much was filled in by his pupils Josef Eybler and Franz Anton Süssmayr—nor how much of Süssmayr's final version was based on Mozart's sketches (some of which he probably destroyed) or his instructions. What is indisputable is the work's unevenness, not in style, like the C minor Mass, but in execution and level of inspiration.

Certainly the opening movement, the Requiem aeternam, with its solemn but very human beauty, is one of the finest, and it sets off the slightly formal double fugue of the Kyrie to excellent effect. These movements' authenticity is proved by the existence of a score in Mozart's own hand (its final page is shown on p. 74). This score (which after the first two movements is largely orchestrated by Eybler) goes as far as the opening of the Lacrimosa, thus including the magnificent music of the Sequence section—the short but very powerful Dies irae, Rex tremendae and Confutatis choruses and the gently grave Recordare. The continuation of the Lacrimosa seems a shade too mechanical to be wholly Mozart's work. But the Offertory is authentic, and although Süssmayr claimed the next three movements (and was almost certainly responsible for the adaptation of music from the opening movements for the closing ones), one suspects at least a touch of Mozart in the main ideas of the Sanctus and the Agnus Dei, and substantially more than that in the sublime Benedictus. All told, the Requiem is hardly worthy to stand, as some have devoutly wished, as his ultimate achievement; but it is nonetheless a work of profoundly impressive spiritual power.

Before moving on to the solo songs, some of Mozart's miscellaneous vocal pieces must be mentioned briefly. Among his masonic compositions are three cantatas [429, 471 and 623] for male voices, music whose general style will remind the listener of *The Magic Flute*. His social music includes some delightful little trios with wind accompaniments, dating from 1783, as well as several canons of varying degrees of bawdiness.

Mozart's solo songs with piano accompaniment number about forty, of which two are in French, one is in Italian and the rest, mostly written in 1784-8, are in German. It would be a mistake to attempt to judge these drawing-room trifles by yardsticks applicable only to the nineteenth-century Lied. Mozart was born too early to be a real Lieder composer. The songs of Schubert and the romantics are different in kind from those of Mozart and his contemporaries—in their more personal attitude to the subject matter, in their much more subtle and highly developed relationship between voice and piano and in the literary worth of the poetry. With a single exception, Mozart's songs are to verse by very minor poets. The exception is *Das Veilchen* [476], to a poem by Goethe, a perfectly shaped miniature with a depth of feeling which suggests a real sense of personal involvement. But there are other songs well worth attention, such as the lyrical and expressive *Abendempfindung* [523], *Luise* [520], a scena telling of a woman burning the letters from her faithless lover, and *Das Lied der Trennung* [519], a lament.

Title-page of a collection of songs for children, including three songs by Mozart (K.596-8)

Finally, a very different type of song, designed for the concert hall or the opera-house rather than the drawing-room—the concert aria. Some were written simply as vehicles for particular singers, some for insertion in other composers' operas. It is on the whole fair to say that anything Mozart did well in the concert arias he did slightly better in his operas: he had more of the factors under his immediate control when setting a text as part of a complete opera than in setting one in isolation, and there is consequently more sense of character and drama.

But it would be misleading to imply that drama is generally lacking in Mozart's concert arias. The three [418-20] written for Anfossi's *Il curioso indiscreto*—the original items did not suit the Viennese singers, one of whom was Aloysia Lange—were clearly conceived to show up Anfossi's inferior dramatic talents, although Mozart openly disclaimed any intention of improving on the Neapolitan maestro. Of the display pieces for special singers, three written during the Mannheim period are of special interest—two for Aloysia, 'Non so d'onde viene' [294], which is almost a declaration of love, and the virtuoso 'Popoli di Tessaglia' [316]; the third, 'Se al labbro mio' [295], was cleverly planned to suit the ageing tenor, Raaff. Possibly Mozart's masterpiece in the field is 'Non temer, amato bene' [505], a scena for soprano (Nancy Storace) with piano obbligato, full of subtle dialogues between voice and instrument. A piece written for Josefa Duschek, at the time of *Don Giovanni*, must also be mentioned ('Bella mia fiamma' [528]): Mozart is said to have been locked in her summer house until it was finished, so by way of revenge he gave her a vocal part full of difficult and awkward intervals, which—with Mozart characteristically making the best of any situation—much enhance the music's dramatic effectiveness.

Mozart's pianoforte (it is now thought that the portrait by Helbling, seen in the background, is not of Mozart)

The Piano and Chamber Music

It is unfortunate that Mozart is so often approached through his piano sonatas. Less rewarding to the young pianist than the keyboard music of Bach, Beethoven or Chopin, they can easily give rise to a mistaken undervaluation of Mozart's worth as a composer. His piano music —as we shall call it, although some of it was first conceived for the harpsichord—should be seen in its proper perspective. Most of it was written for teaching purposes or as drawing-room music for young ladies; the solo keyboard was not the kind of expressive vehicle for Mozart that it was for Beethoven, and while Beethoven's sonatas are rightly seen as occupying a key position in his output and development Mozart's are to be viewed as no more than the by-products of a genius that moved along quite different lines.

The piano sonatas divide neatly into three groups. Of the first set [279-84], the most popular today is the easy G major [283], though the one in E flat [282] has more distinction—its Adagio first movement is a piece for the connoisseur. The next group dates from the time of the journey to Mannheim and Paris. Two sonatas [309 and 311] were written at Mannheim, of which the first, referred to on p. 34, was designed to picture Rosa Cannabich's personality in its Andante. Clearly she was a girl of high sensibility. Much superior is K.310, in A minor, a key Mozart very rarely used. With its purposeful sense of urgency, it is the first of the sonatas which demands to be taken entirely seriously. Mozart did not maintain this manner for the other 1778 sonatas [330-3], the group written in response to Leopold's suggestion that he should adopt a more popular style. His effort here to please the near-beginner is still successful after two centuries. Every embryo pianist knows the F major,

The Mozart Family (oil painting by della Croce, 1780–1)

as well as the A major, which, with its graceful variations and minuet and its Turkish Rondo finale, far transcends the school-room level and often appears on the concert platform.

All the remaining sonatas date from the Viennese period. Two, the supremely popular C major [545] and the B flat [570] are easy teaching pieces which are music to play, not to write about; a third, in F, Mozart put together by adding two new movements [533] to a slightly earlier Rondo [494]. Of more importance are the fiery C minor [457]—in a direct line of succession from K.310, a line which was eventually to lead to Beethoven—and the last Sonata, in D [576], the only one of the Prussian commission to be completed, where elegance suitable to the Potsdam princess combines with the almost symphonic use of counterpoint characteristic of Mozart's late music to produce a work fit to stand at the head of the sonatas.

Of the other piano music, the most important and musically interesting works have already been mentioned (p. 90). The three fantasias [396-7, 475] are the major items; of these K.475, which Mozart published together with the C minor Sonata, is a deeply passionate work, in the fanciful, almost wild emotional style cultivated by C. P. E. Bach, but with genuine formal integrity. Others of this group, all to some extent indebted to C. P. E. Bach, are the highly chromatic Minuet in D [355], the poignant B minor Adagio [540] and the two Rondos [485 and 511]. One particularly fine isolated movement is the little-known Allegro in G minor [312], of uncertain date, a sonata movement full of nervous energy and intensity. These works cover a far wider expressive range than the sonatas, and indeed are the most truly representative section of Mozart's music for solo piano.

The piano variations, of which there are some fifteen sets, can be seen as formalised, written-out versions of Mozart's improvisations. Here the object is to be ingenious and decorative, not to probe deeply into the ultimate possibilities of a theme as did Beethoven or Brahms. The virtuoso element is of prime importance both from the composer's viewpoint, for the expressive range that could be covered, and the performer's, for sheer brilliance of technique.

Three gay early sonatas and two mature ones make up the main works for piano duet. Supreme among them is K.497 in F, which is on a symphonic scale, far more highly developed than the other mature one, K.521. The first movement in particular is masterly, with its subtle use of the dark hues of the minor mode, its semi-contrapuntal second subject and its apparently simple development section, where there is some extremely clever manipulation of musical tensions. The two fantasias in F minor [594 and 608] are nowadays often heard in their piano duet form as well as on the organ. Originally they were written for mechanical organ, an instrument Mozart disliked intensely. One can sense his lack of involvement in the music, even in the soulful A flat Andante of K.608, yet he was too good a musician to do even the most distasteful job badly, and in the force and power of its contrapuntal writing the second Fantasia has a high place in his output. Another contrapuntal *tour de force* is the severe and complex two-piano Fugue in C minor [426], mentioned on p. 86. It could scarcely be less like Mozart's only other two-piano work, the brilliant and extrovert Sonata in D [448].

And so we come to the true chamber music, the music written not for the concert-room but for the amateur to play in his own home—to play, it must be emphasised, rather than to listen to: participation in chamber music is the key to its understanding.

The essence of chamber music, as it is usually seen today, lies in the participation of each of the performers on an equal footing. Mozart's sonatas for piano and violin make an appropriate stepping-stone from the keyboard to true chamber music, since the early ones are little more than piano sonatas with an optional violin accompaniment while the later ones show a gradual development towards equal importance of the two parts.

The sonatas of his childhood [6-15, 26-31] are only of interest to the musical historian and would seem emptily conventional to the ordinary listener. His later ones divide into three groups. First come the seven composed in 1778 at Paris and Mannheim [296, 301-6]. Here again Mozart was concerned with producing light and agreeable works for publication, and five of them are in the popular two-movement form. They vary a good deal in mood, from the typical D major brilliance of K.306 or the expansiveness of K.296 (not included in the published set) to the gentle grace of K.301 and the introspection of K.304. The growing importance of the violin part is seen in the opening bars of the first of the sonatas:

The 'accompanist' does not continue to predominate in this manner, and is often back in his secondary role, but there is more of true dialogue here and it is clear in which direction Mozart was moving, possibly prompted by the Schuster sonatas which had impressed him. Much the most striking of the set is K.304, his only full-length work in E minor. There is a touch of almost romantic passion in the way Mozart handles the first movement's opening theme, presented initially in hollow, bare octaves; and the minuet, with a trio in E major, has a pathetic, wistful air. This is one of Mozart's few ventures into the world of eighteenth-century romantic sensibility, and an entirely successful one.

Eight sonatas [376-80 and 402-4], dating mainly from the early Viennese days, and two unimportant sets of variations [359-60] comprise the next group. K.378, a fairly extended work with a slow movement of particular beauty, is probably rather earlier than the others. It was unusual to include two sonatas in the same key in a set designed for publication, but here there are two in F major [376-7]. Perhaps Mozart felt that the first of them left too many of the key's potentialities unexplored; if so, he certainly repaired the deficiency in K.377, which has an exuberant opening Allegro full of rushing triplets, a variation slow movement in D minor, looking ahead to the string quartet in that key [421], and a minuet finale of surpassing sweetness. K.379 in G suffers from an indifferent set of variations as its finale and in consequence its impassioned G minor Allegro is too little known. The Sonata in E flat [380] is well worth a mention for its singing, if not especially profound, G minor Andante, and for its gay 6/8 finale which looks ahead to the style of the finales of some of the mature piano concertos. K.402-4 are unimportant; they were written for Constanze and all left incomplete.

The final group consists of four sonatas. K.454, in B flat, was not intended for the diversion of amateurs but for performance at a concert where Mozart himself played with the young Italian violinist Regina Strinasacchi. He took full advantage of the consequent freedom in dealing with the relationship of the two instruments, and though the

Manuscript of the Sonata in F, K.377, showing the opening of the minuet

violin still often accompanies this is the first sonata in which there is a sense of true equilibrium between the partners. It is a spacious, brilliant work, especially in the noble sweep of its first movement; yet the chromaticisms of the finale's main theme demonstrate that it is by no means wholly extrovert in mood:

The next sonata, K.481, falls short of the expressive range of K.454, despite a slow movement with some remarkable modulations. But K.526, in A, crowns the series. Though not the last sonata—an unimportant piece, K.547, was to follow—it summarises all Mozart had done in the form. Its first movement, a 6/8 Molto Allegro, shows the subtlest of relationships between the violin and the pianist's two hands and, incidentally, between its themes. The profoundly original Andante contrasts extreme sparseness of texture with richness in harmony and modulation, while the long Presto finale is a moto perpetuo which is high in spirits but never merely vivacious.

It is only a small step from the accompanied sonata to the piano trio, which in Mozart's early days was simply a sonata with two accompany-

Title-page of the first edition of the sonatas K.296, 376–80 (1781)

ing instruments. Mozart wrote only seven complete works in this form. The first, K.254, he called a divertimento, and in some respects it resembles the wind divertimentos of the same period, especially in the gay bustle of its first movement. As in many Haydn piano trios, the cello part is only barely obbligato.

Apart from an unfinished work in D minor [442], Mozart did not return to the form until 1786, the time of *Figaro*, when he wrote three trios within a few months. The instrumental relationships which by this time he had worked out in the violin sonata he applied here, though naturally the cello's participation could not be of the same kind as the violin's. But in the first of these three [496], it takes part in a good deal of dialogue, in the development of the opening Allegro and in the very chromatic slow movement, though it is mainly reduced to drudgery in the variation finale. The next trio [498] is for the unusual combination of clarinet, viola and piano. Written for musical evenings with the Jacquin family, it is a curious but lovable work, starting with an intimate, gentle Andante, rather sombre in colour; the same mood persists in the minuet and rondo, due largely to the similar basic tempos of all the movements and the underlying links between their themes. K.502 is no less of a masterpiece. In its first movement Mozart follows Haydn's practice of using the same material, but differently handled, for his two main subjects:

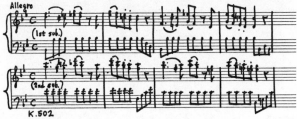

K.502

As the development begins, instead of embarking on further explorations of this idea (it has already been much developed in the exposition) Mozart calmly announces a new, apparently irrelevant theme, ignoring the original one until just before the recapitulation. The slow movement is simple both in design and in its sheer melodic beauty, while the finale is one of those very characteristic movements of a strangely ambivalent nature—a brilliant surface but a touch of pathos not far below.

Yet Mozart's finest work in the form is his next trio, in E major [542], his only work in this key. Slightly withdrawn in feeling, its glories are not easy to describe. One must mention, in the first movement, the cello's passionate entries with the second subject in a distant key and the inexorable logic of the return to tonal normality; and, in the Andante, the utter simplicity of the opening theme and the subtle shadings of emotional significance which the string entries lend it. If the remaining two trios are not on this level, one can hardly complain. The C major [548] never quite justifies the pomp of its start, and is at its best in the playful finale, while the G major [564] signally fails to maintain the promise of its opening bars.

Mozart's chamber music with piano is completed by two quartets and a piano and wind quintet—all three of them works of astonishing perfection, especially considering that the combination of piano and three or more other instruments is not only awkward to handle but had been little explored by Mozart's time. First comes the Quartet in G minor [478], which is as impassioned as Mozart's two other great works in this key; the chromatic harmony of the rondo's opening theme shows that the turn to the major key represents no mere homage before the idol of conventionally cheerful good manners. The second Quartet, in E flat [493] is a more serene and relaxed work, full of soft sunshine, with that kind of easy mastery so obvious in *Figaro* (written at the same time).

'I myself consider it to be the best work I have ever composed,' Mozart wrote of the piano and wind Quintet [452] after its first performance. One may take for granted Mozart's understanding of the limitations of the wind instruments (oboe, clarinet, bassoon and horn), but what is so remarkable is the way he makes a virtue of them, especially in his spontaneous evolution of a thematic style based largely on dialogue and colour contrasts. The consequent shortness of phrases makes the work difficult to perform satisfactorily, but that scarcely diminishes its stature.

In the field of chamber music without piano, pride of place must naturally go to the string quartet, if only on quantitative grounds. Besides the early Sammartini-like quartet [80] written at Lodi, he composed twelve quartets in 1772-3 as well as the ten 'celebrated' quartets in Vienna. The first six [155-60], written during the last visit to Italy, are short and lightweight works, without as yet the highly developed relationship between instruments which Mozart was to learn from Joseph Haydn and other Viennese composers. The works in G [156] and B flat [159] stand out, the former for its perfectly shaped opening Presto and its deeply felt E minor Adagio, the latter for the easy grace of its opening Andante, its forceful G minor Allegro and witty rondo.

Features of the next group [168-73] have already been discussed (p. 84), and no recapitulation is needed here. But it is worth drawing attention to the two outstanding quartets of the set. While K.169 and 172 have leanings towards the Italian symphonic style, and K.168 and 170 incline no less towards Haydn, there is more individuality in K.171 —its sonata-form first movement has contrapuntal propensities, and there is a sombre C minor slow movement—and most of all in K.173, in D minor. Its elaborate final fugue, perhaps, is not really Mozartean, but in the first movement and the minuet (separated by a graceful gavotte) there is much of the feeling of tragedy and protest which one associates with his later use of the key.

The last ten quartets comprise the set of six dedicated to Haydn, a single work written for the publisher Hoffmeister and the three designed for the cello-playing Prussian monarch. Mozart is seen at his most personal in the Haydn set. One is always aware that this is not music for public performance or other exhibition purposes; it was written as music for the connoisseur—the quartet-playing amateur was the connoisseur then, and remains so—and for the ultimate connoisseur of string quartets, Joseph Haydn himself.

There can be no question here of singling out for discussion the most characteristic, or the best, of the series: each work is too individual and most of them are superlative. To the average music-lover, it is probably the D minor [421] which will impress most readily. The restrained passion of its *sotto voce* opening, the abrupt *fortes* and *pianos*, the deliberate discontinuity of line, the chromaticisms, the juxtapositions of emptiness and warmth in the development, and finally the poignancy of the second subject when heard in the minor—all these add up to make a movement of intense effectiveness. There is a strong, impassioned minuet, with a sublime major-key trio, and a variation finale modelled on a Haydn movement (as we saw on p. 84) but with an extra dimension of pathos.

The G major [387] has already been mentioned for its use of fugue within a sonata-type formal plan—in its finale, for in a first movement

Manuscript of the String Quartet in D minor, K.421, showing the opening

such frivolities could not be countenanced. K.428 in E flat is more intro-verted than most of Mozart's works in the key; no other E flat work has an opening of such mystery:

or, continuing the chromatic flavour, has such a *Tristan*-esque passage as this:

Although the minuet's first bars may derive from Haydn (as we saw on p. 84) the trio is entirely Mozartean: while Haydn's trios often have a rustic, hearty element, Mozart's nearly always move towards greater refinement. K.458 in B flat (the *Hunt*) is the gayest of the set, at least on a superficial level, and probably the least remarkable.

Leopold's observation that the last three were 'somewhat lighter' certainly applies to K.458, but less certainly to the other two, where possibly art conceals art more subtly. K.464, in A, has a first movement of exemplary structural clarity, with rather a long development section, and its minuet too is elaborately developed. The slow movement is a set of variations, and it is interesting to see how, as in K.421, Mozart has retained something from the primitive variation technique of giving each of the players a turn in the limelight; yet this elementary method is harnessed to profoundly expressive ends, a far cry from its employment in exhibition pieces by lesser composers. The finale is another miracle of concise construction—one usually learns that Haydn or Beethoven, not Mozart, could build up movements from no more than a thematic germ, but this poetic and faintly melancholy movement is almost entirely based on the two figures of its opening theme:

The famous *Dissonance* Quartet [465], with its notorious chromatic slow introduction, concludes the set in the imperious style—often jubilant and high-spirited, but never shallow—which Mozart so often used in C major works.

The *Hoffmeister* Quartet [499] forms a kind of pendant to the Haydn set. Its first movement embodies some of Mozart's most exquisite quartet writing, notably towards the ends of the exposition and recapitulation sections, where there are some poetic distant modulations. The minuet, with its high viola part, has an almost Boccherinian luxuriance of texture. In the slowly unfolding Adagio the lengths are only heavenly, and there is a finale full of surprises.

A special problem was posed by the last three quartets [575, 589-90]: how to reconcile the requirements of a cellist king with the integrity of true string quartet style. There is no real solution, as Mozart of course knew. A good share of the melodic material had to be given to the cello and its routine accompanying had to be made interesting, with the net result that Mozart was forced to discard the very means that enabled him to reach such heights in the seven previous quartets. And Friedrich Wilhelm was a less inspiring dedicatee than Joseph Haydn.

In Mozart's time the string quintet form was rare. Joseph Haydn wrote none, Michael Haydn a few; the only other major figure to use the form was Luigi Boccherini, but his hundred or so string quintets are all for two violins, one viola and two cellos, the first cello part clearly conceived with his own virtuoso playing in mind. Mozart's six quintets, like Michael Haydn's, have an extra viola rather than an extra cello, forming a combination much easier to handle and musically more satisfactory, as far as Mozart's style was concerned.

Title-page of the first edition of Mozart's six string quartets dedicated to Haydn

His first quintet [174] dates from 1773, the same time as the second set of quartets, and is a long, elaborate work, in which he clearly revelled in the textural richness afforded by the extra instrument. Strictly speaking his next quintet is K.406 in C minor, but this work started life as a wind serenade and will later be discussed as such.

The pair in C and G minor [515 and 516] are often paralleled with the *Jupiter* and G minor symphonies. K.515's expansive opening, with its leisurely harmonic rhythm, makes it clear that this is a work on a grand scale. Naturally there is an elaborate development here, but the long coda is exceptional. Second comes the minuet, which is quiet and restrained almost to the point of diffidence—for once the trio section is the emotional centre of gravity. The Andante is a sublime love-duet between first violin and first viola, and the finale is one of those super-ficially gay movements whose sadness lies too deep to be made explicit.

But the sadness of the G minor is of a very different kind, bordering on despair, and explicit enough for the least percipient listener. The G minor Quintet is often seen as Mozart's most personal utterance in any field, and indeed not even the G minor Symphony, for all the tragedy that one may find in it, has such a powerful emotional effect. As in K.515, the minuet (with a major-key trio providing a moment of repose) lies second, preceding the E flat Adagio, a movement both profoundly calm and profoundly disturbing. The finale is in G major, and Mozart naturally provided it with a slow introduction in G minor to help bridge the gulf, tonal and emotional, from the Adagio. With its 6/8 rhythm and major tonality, the finale may seem something of an anticlimax, but its sharp accents and its flirtations with chromaticism and counterpoint can, in a perceptive enough performance, keep it almost on the high plane of the rest of the work.

The other two quintets are late works, and although they are not on the exalted level of K.515-6 they are superior to the late quartets and are undeniably great. K.593, in D, shows Mozart's growing contrapuntal inclinations in his last years—in the first movement (and not only its development), in the canonic passages of the minuet, and above all in the finale, where an apparently innocent theme becomes part of a fabric of quintuple counterpoint. Except in the deeply poetic Adagio, there is something of a return to Haydn's influence, and this applies still more to the last Quintet [614], in E flat, where the finale's opening theme is more typical of Haydn than of Mozart:

In Haydn's manner, too, the trio moves decisively towards the popular rather than the sophisticated, and a slightly 'cheery', extrovert vein runs through the other movements; yet the whole work has an ease of utterance, and the slow movement a beauty and purity, which are never less than Mozartean.

At the head of the miscellaneous chamber works stands Mozart's only string trio, the misnamed Divertimento in E flat [563]. No doubt Mozart called it by the then old-fashioned title because, like a well-behaved divertimento, it had six movements, including two minuets. It is a large-scale masterpiece and a veritable compendium of string trio style. The two string duos [423-4] do all that can be done within the medium, making a virtue of its textural limitations; a little two-movement Trio in B flat for two violins and cello [266], which contemporary convention would probably have called a 'notturno', is his only other string chamber music.

Mozart catered for all the 'indoor' wind instruments in his works for wind and strings. Of the flute quartets, only K.285 needs to be taken at all seriously—an attractive miniature, though not very far beyond what other flute quartet writers achieved. K.298 is a kind of musical joke, with its quotations of other composers and technical crudities, which today may leave most of us unamused, or perhaps smiling for the wrong reasons. But the oboe Quartet [370] is a fine piece, full of tunes that are conceived entirely in terms of oboe tone. An entertaining episode occurs in the finale, where the oboist has a change of rhythm, with 2/4 semiquavers against the strings' 6/8 accompaniment. The humble bassoonist must be content with a little Sonata [292] with cello, but hornists, besides a set of duos [487] (invaluable for practice à 2), have a Quintet [407] with violin, two violas and cello, a light-hearted but beautifully written work. And if the flautist and oboist can find such a thing as a glass harmonica, as well as a viola and cello, there is some very satisfying music for them in the Adagio and Rondo [617].

Last, the clarinettist, who is much the most fortunate—for his instrument, in Anton Stadler's hands, inspired not only the Trio mentioned on p. 106 and the Concerto [622], but the Quintet in A [581]. It is perhaps being wise after the event to speak of the autumnal quality of this work's mellow beauty. In the earlier works for wind and strings, all written before Mozart reached a true chamber-music style, the concertante relationship between one instrument and the others provided no special problems. But by this time it did; and how Mozart nevertheless produced a work of true chamber music integrity and immaculate form is one of those creative miracles which, although we can analyse it, can only be explained by resort to the word 'genius'.

Mozart (engraving after a boxwood medallion by Posch, 1789)

Entertainment Music

All Mozart's music is basically entertainment music. What distinguishes the material of this section from the rest is that it was not written for an audience to listen to, more or less attentively, but was designed as a pleasant background to other activities. When we sit in a concert hall, listening in solemn silence to an eighteenth-century serenade or divertimento, we should realise that the music was never intended to bear such a weight of concentration. It was meant simply as a decorative addition to other pleasures—like talking, eating, drinking or love-making—of a highly sophisticated society.

Most of Mozart's works of this kind fall under the headings of serenade or divertimento. Another class of his entertainment music, though, deserves to be spared a few lines—his dance music. Mozart wrote nearly two hundred dances, more than half of them minuets, the remainder German Dances and contredanses. This was not background music, but purely functional: unlike Bach's allemandes or Chopin's mazurkas, Mozart's dances were written for the sole purpose of being danced to, mostly at court balls, for which he was obliged to provide music from 1787 onwards in his capacity as court chamber musician. Features of the dances are Mozart's varied and colourful handling of the orchestra and his inexhaustible melodic fertility. To Mozart himself, their composition was no more than a hack job, but even so many of them are as felicitous as they are unknown.

The works of the serenade and divertimento type can be divided into three groups, by their style rather than their titles, for terms like divertimento, serenade, cassation, finalmusik and notturno carried their own inflections but had no really precise meaning for eighteenth-century

Manuscript of a Contredanse, K.609 No. 1, which Mozart arranged from 'Non più andrai' from 'The Marriage of Figaro'

composers. Excluding one category—the music for wind instruments alone, to be discussed first—Mozart's output here can be roughly divided into works requiring only small resources and tending to a chamber music style, and works for full orchestra inclining towards the symphony or concerto. Mozart mostly used the title 'divertimento' for the former type and 'serenade' for the latter.

Most of the wind music is fairly early. Two divertimentos [187-8] are notable only for their extraordinary combination of instruments, two flutes, five trumpets and four drums. They were designed for some military occasion in Salzburg when such a band was available. Probably written for performance in Milan or Munich in the early 1770s are four more divertimentos: two [196e-f] for pairs of oboes, clarinets, bassoons and horns, and two [166 and 186] for the same with the addition of a pair of cors anglais. Rather more polished than these are the six composed in Salzburg between 1775 and 1777, for oboes, bassoons and horns (there were no clarinets in the Salzburg establishment). They are simple, light-hearted and unpretentious, ideal background music for a warm summer evening. K.270 is the most fluent and finished of this group, K.289 so much the weakest that its authenticity may be doubted (as can that of K. 196e and f).

116

The later wind music, however, is more than merely entertaining. K.361, a serenade for thirteen instruments—the usual eight with two extra horns, two basset-horns and a double-bass—is on a magnificent scale. Probably it was written for the Munich orchestra at the time of *Idomeneo*. Part of its fascination lies in the sheer beauty of its sound. In the first movement, Mozart uses the available combinations of instruments almost kaleidoscopically—clarinets and bassoons, basset-horns and bassoons, oboes and basset-horns, and many other permutations. But the real marvel of sensuous tonal beauty is the Adagio, where various instruments in turn serenade the listener through the warm, fragrant luxuriance of the background texture. There are seven movements in all, including two minuets (each with two trios), a Romanze almost overflowing with sentiment, and a set of variations where again Mozart exploits in highly poetic fashion the rich variety of colour available from the thirteen instruments.

Two serenades for eight instruments were written just after K.361. K.375, in E flat, was originally without oboes, and the use of the standard military band combination of the period led Mozart to adopt a somewhat martial and open-air style. He wrote it 'rather carefully', he said, as an influential court chamberlain was to hear it. On his name-day in 1781 a group of players came to the courtyard of his house, just as he was going to bed, and 'in the most pleasant fashion imaginable' serenaded him with this work. Mozart's last wind serenade is in C minor [388], and is a work of a very different kind, as much for the chamber as for the open air, a point emphasised by its having four movements as opposed to K.375's five. Its dark, impassioned nature, its fiercely aggressive outbursts, its sense of urgency ·which underlies even the lyrical sections—these mark it as a work of much more serious intent. The canonic minuet and doubly canonic trio, and the variation finale, less bent on exploitation of tone-colour than the variations of K.361, maintain the first movement's uncompromising mood. Mozart later raised the work's social status by arranging it as a string quintet, but this version softens the music's firm outlines.

The only remaining wind music comprises some divertimentos probably written for three basset-horns, now generally played on two clarinets and bassoon [439b]—pleasant miniatures, intended more for playing (probably in the Jacquin circle) than listening to—and also a canon for two basset-horns and bassoon [410], a solemnly beautiful Adagio for two clarinets and three basset-horns [411] and a poignant fragmentary Adagio [580a] probably for clarinet and three basset-horns.

Of the works tending to chamber rather than orchestral music, calling for solo string players rather than an orchestra, the earliest is an easy-going Divertimento in D [205], probably written in Vienna and, especially in the slightly bucolic quality of its two minuets, showing signs of Joseph Haydn's influence. More sophisticated in style is another Divertimento in D [251], for oboe, horns and strings. There is a quality of poise and elegance about this work which, together with the use of the oboe and the 'alla francese' march, has led commentators to suggest French influence. (Most divertimentos and serenades have a march associated with them, for use as an introduction and/or conclusion.)

Also written in Salzburg were three divertimentos [247, 287 and 334] for strings and two horns—the horns do little more than help sustain the harmony and reinforce the tuttis, but they add a fulness and round-ness to the texture, giving the works a special colour. Unlike true chamber music, the relationship between parts is far from equal: the first violinist has to cope with brilliant concerto-like writing while the bass occupies a somewhat menial role. Free from the constraints which a strict chamber music style imposed, he produced music of a refreshing, gracefully witty and relaxed quality which must have enhanced the occasions (two of them evenings at the home of Countess Lodron) for which they were written. Each is in six movements, including two minuets and two slow movements, one of them usually in variation form, which gave Mozart plenty of opportunities to explore the range of emotions suitable to purely social music.

The near-chamber music category concludes with two much later works, entitled *Ein Musikalischer Spass* (*A Musical Joke*) [522], for strings and horns, and *Eine Kleine Nachtmusik* (*A Little Nocturne*) [525], for strings. Much of the broad humour of the *Musical Joke* is lost today, except perhaps on musicologists who know what bad eighteenth-century music is like or on teachers of composition who know the elementary faults. To the normal music-lover, the joke is likely to mis-fire. The famous *Eine Kleine Nachtmusik* rounds off this series with a perfect reconciliation between the demands of Mozart's mature style and the limitations of light music. With the concertante style of string writing long behind him, it is impossible to tell from its absence here whether the work was intended for solo instruments or orchestra; but for the same reasons it is equally effective either way, as long as the full weight of a modern symphony orchestra is not used. There were originally five movements to the *Kleine Nachtmusik*, but the pages of Mozart's manuscript bearing the first minuet were torn out—possibly, as Einstein has suggested, a minuet in a doubtful piano sonata [Anh. 136] is a transposed arrangement of it.

Just as the divertimentos considered above are like chamber music in a less concentrated form, so the remaining works are like less concentrated symphonies or concertos. The first three [63, 99 and 100], sometimes called 'cassations', date from Mozart's fourteenth year and were written for festive occasions in Salzburg—large-scale works, one of them in as many as eight movements, appropriately gay in mood. Next is an isolated four-movement piece [113] written in Milan, more intimate in style, and using clarinets for the first time; Mozart entitled it 'Concerto ò sia Divertimento', perhaps because of its concerto-like contrasts between wind and strings. For strings alone are three effervescent

Wind band of the Prince of Oettingen-Wallerstein, 1791

divertimentos [136-8], each in three movements, which are among the most polished productions of his youth. Sometimes they are called the 'Salzburg Symphonies' and sometimes they are classed among the quartets. With no more of the chamber music atmosphere than that of the full-dress concert-hall occasion, they do not really fit into either category.

A feature of the next Divertimento [131] is the enterprisingly witty writing for four horns, as opposed to the customary two. It is in D major, always the favourite key for festive music, as it is the most sonorous and brilliant key for strings, and the best for trumpets. In the same key and the same number of movements (seven) is a Finalmusik [185]. Written during the 1773 Vienna visit for nameday festivities in a Salzburg family, it is typical of Austrian serenade music, gay and robust yet often tender. Like the pair of serenades [203-4] which followed during the next two summers, possibly written for the celebrations on Colloredo's name-days, K.185 incorporates a violin concerto. In each of these three, the leader of the orchestra is required to show his paces in an Andante and an Allegro on the scale of a small concerto, and in the trio of one of the minuets. These miniature concertos are almost works in themselves, as well as being parts of larger works; in K.185 and K.203 they are even in keys foreign to those of the other movements.

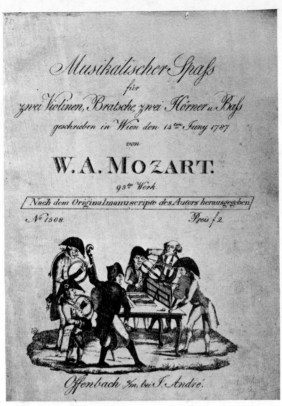

Title-page of
the first edition
of the 'Musical
Joke', K.522

Two smaller serenades, each in three movements, date from 1776-7. First of these is the *Serenata Notturna* [239], in which a concertante group of two violins, viola and double-bass is set against an orchestra of strings and timpani. The interplay between solo ensemble and orchestra is very subtly handled and the resulting euphony is one of the work's special charms. Its first movement is a march, with the pompous dotted rhythms of the tuttis set off by more lyrical phrases for the soloists; next is a minuet, again a mixture of pomp and elegance, with a trio for the soloists alone; and finally there is a sparkling rondo, with a mock-solemn Adagio in the middle leading to a particularly jaunty episode. K.286, a Notturno for four orchestras, each of strings and horns, is based entirely on echo effects, and is not on the same inventive level.

The last two serenades for full orchestra are the *Haffner* [250], written for wedding festivities in the Salzburg family of that name, and the *Posthorn* [320], both in D. With three minuets, one of them between the Andante and the Rondeau of the violin concerto, the *Haffner* is another large-scale work. Its first movement is truly symphonic in character, without infringing the limitations on seriousness which are imposed by good manners at wedding celebrations. The Rondeau, with its delicious tripping semiquavers, has rightly become something of a violinists' party piece. Last, the *Posthorn*, written shortly after Mozart's return from Paris and Mannheim and showing much of the newly acquired brilliance and forcefulness of orchestral style. Here the interpolated concerto is not for violin but for wind instruments, a sort of Sinfonia Concertante in two movements for pairs of flutes, oboes and bassoons. The posthorn of the title is used in one of the trios to the second minuet.

A grand finale to the series is the *Haffner* Symphony [385], which Mozart originally wrote as a five-movement serenade. We have seen how he was gradually moving towards a more symphonic musical language; and when, in 1782, he wrote the *Haffner* Symphony, he had reached a stage of his development at which he could no longer express himself by means of the leisurely and relatively diffuse serenade style. There are still serenade elements in this work which one does not find in Mozart's other symphonies, but the opposite way of saying the same thing is more significant—there are sufficient symphonic elements in this work, conceived as a serenade, to make it a splendid symphony; and that was something new. So at this point we leave the delights of serenading to embark on the more serious business of the symphony.

Carl Friedrich Abel (after an oil painting by Gainsborough)

The Symphonies

While in Mozart's time chamber music was meant for playing, and the serenade for half-hearing, the symphony was music for listening to. The primary purpose, entertainment, still remained. Like Beethoven or Brahms, Mozart wrote his symphonies with a view to public consumption, to show the world what he could do; but unlike them, he did not attempt to embody any kind of spiritual message in his symphonies. He aimed to send the audience home happy, not enlightened or morally uplifted.

Altogether Mozart wrote some fifty symphonies. The traditional numbering, up to 41, includes some which are spurious, excludes several which are authentic and confuses the order of many more. As those up to No. 30 [202] (in fact the 39th) throw a good deal of light on Mozart's development it is important to see their correct chronology, which is shown in the list on p. 178.

Mozart wrote his first symphony [16] when he was nine. Its outstanding feature is not so much the thematic invention, which is ordinary, nor even the harmony and orchestration, though they are clever enough for a boy of nine, but its overall form and style, demonstrating Mozart's astonishing grasp of the Italianate symphonic manner which he had just encountered in the music of J. C. Bach and C. F. Abel. The next symphony, K.19, shows a quite extraordinary musical advance, and apart from an occasional tautological passage and some short-winded phrases the first movement could well pass as genuine J. C. Bach, especially in its characteristic *forte-piano* alternations, while the Andante is no less in his manner. K.22 is similar in style, with a J. C. Bach reminiscence as its finale's main theme (see p. 80).

The first three symphonies have only three movements each, but the next six, dating from the 1767 visit to Vienna, reflect current Viennese taste by including minuets. K.43 in F begins with a phrase borrowed from Abel and has some *opera buffa* elements, but there is definite progress here towards the more highly developed Viennese style. In the slow movement, adapted from a duet in *Apollo et Hyacinthus* [38], there is some delicate and charming scoring, while the gigue-like finale has more symphonic feeling than previous movements of the kind. Particularly Viennese in style is K.48 in D: the wind instruments are more carefully handled here to enrich the texture, and the first movement is in full sonata form. The almost unbroken tutti scoring in this bustling Allegro contrasts strongly with the somewhat meek Andante for strings alone.

During the long first journey to Italy Mozart wrote five symphonies. Typically, he adopted here the lightweight Italian manner. The three written at Rome [81, 97 and 95], in particular, are frothy little pieces, clear and brilliant in effect but extremely insubstantial. K.84, in D major like the Roman three, was composed at Milan and Bologna and has slightly more substance. Its opening theme gives a good idea of the fanfare-like brilliance Mozart was aiming at, and its second subject is no less typical of the light, tripping melodies he used for contrast:

K.74 in G, written in Milan on the way home, is rather different—some of the southern glitter is still there but the treatment of themes and especially the more elaborate orchestral texture with frequent solo passages for the oboes argues a move back towards the Viennese type. There is no break between the first two movements, and the Rondeau finale is full of wit, with some very unexpected modulations. Probably all these were in three movements at first, the minuets in two of the Rome group being later additions.

The symphonies written during the few months at Salzburg are a little more weighty in style. K.73, in C, has a good measure of high spirits along with slightly old-fashioned pseudo-contrapuntal passages. It has a very charming slow movement, with flutes, as well as a pompous minuet and an unsophisticated finale. Possibly Austrian influence, specifically that of the Haydn brothers, is seen here and in K.75. In the latter Mozart experimented with uneven phrase-lengths in the minuet and finale, and the orchestral texture is a good deal more carefully planned than usual, with imitative passages between the violins, even occasionally involving the violas, and melodic material on the oboes.

K.110 is similar in style; its slow movement has important bassoon parts and the minuet is canonic, like several of Haydn's.

Three more symphonies followed in 1771: a ceremonious and richly-scored work in C [96], with a C minor Andante full of sharply alternating *piano* and *forte* marks; a gay one in F [112], with a triple-time opening movement full of drive; and the first of his symphonies in A [114], with a notably fine minuet and, rather exceptionally, using oboes in the slow movement but flutes otherwise (the opposite way round was more common). Although the first two were written in Milan, and *buffo* elements are present, Mozart's general leanings towards the Viennese style are still pronounced. About this time he added a Presto [120] to the very Italianate two-movement overture to *Ascanio in Alba*, so as to turn it into a symphony. Such interchange between theatre and concert-room was quite usual—Mozart later did the same for three other opera overtures, while earlier he had cut the minuet of Symphony No. 7 [45] so as to use it as a three-movement overture to *La finta semplice*.

The next seven symphonies, Nos. 15-21, were written at Salzburg during 1772. They include works which could be said to summarise all the lines of development Mozart was following, with added strength of invention and richness of treatment: K.129 in G, a three-movement work, recalls the J. C. Bach type, K.133 in D is more in the brilliant Italian style, while K.124 and 128 have stronger leanings towards Haydn. K.130 in F, scored with flutes and two pairs of horns, is notable for a long finale almost as weighty as the first movement—a landmark on the trail that was to lead to the *Jupiter*. The next symphony, K.132 in E flat, has a fine first movement looking ahead in style to several later works in the same key. Mozart wrote alternative slow movements for this work, of which the first is much the more imaginative. There is some canonic writing in the minuet and the trio is full of harmonic surprises; but the symphony's biggest surprise is its very untypical finale, an unsophisticated rondo in gavotte rhythm. K.134 in A is the best work in the group. Although the first movement reverts to semi-sonata form (others, notably K.133, have formal irregularities), it is tersely organised and recalls Haydn, even mature Haydn, in the unorthodoxy of its recapitulation. The Andante, starting with a favourite Mozartean tag

is elegant but deeply felt, and after a boisterous minuet and quietly witty trio the finale manages to be quite symphonic as well as high-spirited.

K.134 is a masterpiece on its own limited scale, but with the 1773-4 symphonies we approach Mozart's first undoubted masterpieces. The beginning of this series of eight works is unimpressive: written just after the last Italian tour, K.162 and 181 are pompous and rather empty, and K.182 is only a little more inventive. Like these, K.199 has Italian leanings—the opening of the first movement development is wholly in the *opera buffa* atmosphere—but the work as a whole has greater life and substance. K.184 in E flat, No. 26, is on a different level. Scored more fully than Mozart's previous symphonies, with flutes, oboes, bassoons, horns and trumpets, it has a first movement full of drama and urgency, with abrupt accents, sharp dynamic contrasts, fierce unison scale passages, tense syncopated rhythms and unexpected chromaticisms. This symphony is in the old Italian overture form, with no breaks between movements: the first leads directly into the attractive, slightly sombre C minor Andante, which in turn leads into the finale, a 3/8 Presto with some rich and elaborate scoring, well worthy of what has gone before.

Mozart wrote the other three symphonies of this group after his Viennese stay. The first and most Haydn-like is No. 28 [200], a C major symphony but without the ceremonial trappings previously associated with the key. Its first movement has a real sense of organic symphonic growth from small germs of thematic material. The Andante is simple —basically just one long violin melody—and the minuet is very much in Haydn's manner. More typically Mozartean is the finale, where Italian-ate sparkle and brilliance are absorbed into a fundamentally Viennese language.

No. 25 [183], the 'little' G minor, is more generally recognised as characteristic. It is easy to read too much, in the way of romantic significance, into this passionate work. The personal part of its nature is actually the better appreciated when one realises that it is just one of a corpus of stormy G minor symphonies, contributed to by men like Vanhal, J. C. Bach and Haydn, all written about the same time. This in no way detracts from its individuality or, of course, its intense effectiveness. Full of subtle thematic relationships which lend it inner unity, it also has many telling but more obvious effects (obvious, that is, once Mozart has thought of them), like the balm of the G major trio, for wind alone, after the storm and stress of the minuet.

The A major Symphony, No. 29 [201] is just as personal. Like many great works, its essential character is elusive—one can equally find in it a sense of sunny contentment or one of impassioned striving. In its attention to detail and its heightened expressive intensity the first movement has something of a chamber music atmosphere. It is interesting that the development uses new material, only tenuously connected with what has gone before. Simple melodic beauty is the slow movement's main feature; the minuet, based on dotted rhythms, is both delicate and sturdy, with a lyrical trio; and the finale tends to be rumbustious, though it has wit and grace, and its development section is unusually dramatic. Although the later movements do not quite equal the first in individuality or musical distinction, the work as a whole is

A page from the first edition of the 'Paris' Symphony, K.297, showing the alternative slow movement

remarkably satisfying and would be a fitting conclusion to Mozart's early symphonies. In fact the series ends with No. 30 in D [202], a work rather divertimento-like in style with many incidental charms and clear leanings to Haydn, but much inferior in inventive power to the three just discussed. Its minuet is the strongest movement.

From mid-1774 to mid-1778 Mozart wrote no symphonies—there was no need to write them unless he was travelling, or contemplating travelling, as they were not normally required of him at Salzburg. His next was No. 31 in D [297], the *Paris*, written for performance in the

French capital. Faced by the necessity of pleasing a new kind of public, he produced a work which is not entirely typical: he donned full dress clothes here, one might say, and they did not fit exactly. The manuscript, with many cuts and alterations, shows that he did not take naturally to the Parisian style. He was both amused and irritated by the Parisian requirements, especially the opening *coup d'archet*, which in fact he almost guyed, making it only four bars long and following it with a long *piano* passage. But if he was prepared to cock a snook at the Parisians he was also prepared to accommodate himself to meet their taste. The brilliant string writing, with rushing scale passages, the exciting crescendos, the obvious delight he took in the rich sound of a woodwind ensemble with clarinets as well as flutes, oboes and bassoons—all these give the work its own special flavour. He was accommodating over the slow movement too, providing a simpler one when Le Gros found the original (the one played today) too elaborate.

Mozart wrote another symphony in Paris, which has not survived—it is certainly not the pathetically feeble overture in B flat [311a] sometimes attributed to him. Back in Salzburg, three more symphonies soon followed. No. 32 in G [318] is a reversion to the Italian overture form (it may have been intended for the unfinished Singspiel *Zaïde*) with the last section a continuation of the first, on the same material. Clearly Mozart was at pains in this dashing little work to show the Salzburgers what he had learnt about orchestral style in Mannheim and Paris. In strong contrast, No. 33 in B flat [319] is particularly endearing for its gentle, chamber music-like qualities, with much attractive oboe and bassoon writing. The first movement has the typical rhythmic momentum of triple-time Allegros, and it shares a formal oddity with the second and fourth movements—instead of a development section there is a kind of episode on new material (including, in the first movement, the *Credo-Jupiter* figure quoted on pp. 88 and 94). In the second, where the episode is less convincingly unified with the rest of the movement, the recapitulation is reversed, the second subject being presented before the first (a favourite device at Mannheim, which Mozart used in two other works of the period, a violin Sonata [306] and a piano Sonata [311]).

In both Nos. 33 and 34 [338] the minuets were later additions; with its concertante wind writing, that of No. 34 does not integrate very satisfactorily with its symphony. Apart from the very graceful slow movement, which is of the continuous violin melody type, No. 34 returns to the ceremonial C major manner, now much enriched by Mozart's growth in sheer musical inventiveness, especially evident in the stride and grandeur of the tuttis. Here again the first movement 'development' is more like an interlude, this time with a slightly mysterious operatic atmosphere and partly in a very remote key, all imaginatively designed to set off the brilliance and straightforwardness of the rest of the movement.

Mozart's 35th Symphony, the *Haffner* [385], stands between symphony and serenade, as we have seen. The flowing sweetness of the Andante and the four-square simplicity of the minuet are obvious serenade elements, and the extrovert nature of the first movement might equally suggest the serenade style. But here there is a hard core of symphonic thought, for all the material is built round the opening figure:

The *Linz* Symphony, No. 36 in C [425], bears some signs of the haste in which it was written. One is the relative exactness of the recapitulations, and another, less obvious, is Mozart's use of Haydn's symphonic style as his starting-point. No doubt it was Haydn's example that led him to write his first symphonic slow introduction; in the Andante he used an opening like Haydn as a springboard for his own invention (with a touch of Michael Haydn in the middle, as we saw on p. 86); and in the minuet, especially its Ländler-like trio, he is very close to Haydn in treatment if not in spirit. But the broad sweep of the first movement

A view of Linz

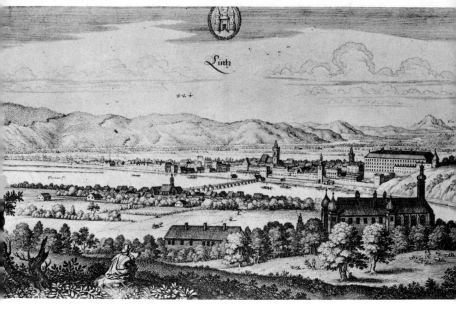

tuttis shows Mozart in his most personally majestic manner while the finale, for all its subtle varieties of texture, including a lot of pseudo-counterpoint, is one of the most polished examples of Mozartean wit.

At the end of 1786, after three years, Mozart returned to the symphony, writing No. 38 in D [504] for his first visit to Prague. We are now in the realm of highly individual and distinctive masterpieces, still designed as entertainment music, but moving closer in spirit to the Beethovenian and romantic concept of the symphony. The *Prague* Symphony has a dark, brooding slow introduction before the main Allegro. Apart from the lyrical second subject, the material of the first movement is designed more for development along contrapuntal lines than for melodic attractiveness, and the movement is consequently one of Mozart's strongest and most powerful. Its form too is of the highest subtlety, especially in the handling of the different versions of the opening theme, with their irregularities in the recapitulation, much akin to those used later by Haydn. Indeed, this recapitulation is among Mozart's most inspired sections, with its poetic modulation to B flat (bar 221), the great climax some twenty bars later and the still greater one at bar 283. No comment is needed on the Andante, serenade-like in its flowing beauty but on a far nobler level. The finale—there is no minuet—is largely constructed from a four-note motif and again shows, particularly in the climactic development section, the significance Mozart was by now attaching to contrapuntal processes.

Indulging in half- or perhaps quarter-truths, the moods of the last three symphonies can be summarised as lyrical, tragic and triumphant. No. 39 in E flat [543]—with its orchestral colouring softened by the use of clarinets in place of the usual oboes—does not begin as a lyrical work, but with an Adagio introduction of a statuesque solemnity looking ahead to *The Magic Flute*. Although much of the 3/4 Allegro is scored for full orchestra, the overall mood is one of tender, smiling grace. The A flat slow movement is almost a soliloquy on one simple lyrical theme, which is presented in a variety of guises, with occasional passionate orchestral outbursts. The minuet is more formal, less intimate, in mood, with a trio whose clarinet melody is like a sophisticated version of Haydn's 'peasant' vein. Again, a single thematic idea is the mainspring of the finale, though the movement is not assertively contrapuntal. This little seven-note tag may seem no more than light-hearted, but its

appearances on the flute and bassoon during the magical 'Neapolitan' modulations of the second subject become almost sinister. And it maintains its surprises to the end.

A page from Mozart's thematic catalogue, showing the last two symphonies

No. 40 [550], the G minor, is probably Mozart's best known symphony. Certainly it is his most accessible, particularly because its essentially personal and perhaps tragic nature is obvious to most listeners. It would be unwise to attempt to relate it too closely to biographical circumstances, especially as works of such varied natures came from Mozart's pen at this period. Even so, one feels that such a work must involve a deep level of human experience. Despite the heartfelt tranquillity of the Andante, and the moment of repose afforded by the G major trio of the minuet, a mood of stress and urgency permeates the symphony from the opening bars (with their throbbing viola background) to the close of the extraordinary finale—extraordinary for the fierce counterpoint and fantastic treatment of tonality in its development section, and for its unremitting energy and tension. Possibly Mozart was prepared to compromise in the G minor Quintet, but here there was no escape from reality, however harsh.

And so to the crowning glories of the *Jupiter* [551]. It is certainly a fitting climax to the symphonies in that it represents a comprehensive drawing-together of threads from all directions. With an added depth and significance, the first movement glances back to the *forte-piano* alternations of J. C. Bach in its opening bars, the pompous C major style in many of its tuttis, and even to *opera buffa* in the second theme of the second subject. The intense richness of the Andante, in woodwind writing and in harmony, and above all the contrapuntal finale, represent a consummation of Viennese symphonic tendencies. It is the finale which is of outstanding interest and importance. This movement is not of course a fugue, but a sonata form movement involving fugal and other kinds of contrapuntal treatment. As we have seen, fugal processes were not new to the symphony, nor were contrapuntal development sections —and in any case novelty is no virtue in itself. But the great contrapuntal climax in the coda, where all the movement's themes are combined, was not merely new but a surpassing stroke of genius for its overwhelming brilliance of effect. As this climactic passage brings the noble series of symphonies to a splendid conclusion, it may also provide the last word in our humble discussion of them:

Ticket of admission to a concert given by Mozart

The Concertos

Wagner or Verdi may have written more great operas than Mozart; Haydn or Beethoven may have written more great quartets or symphonies. But in the field of the concerto Mozart stands unsurpassed as regards both quantity and quality. From his earliest days the form had fascinated him. However, the problems of design, texture and solo-tutti relationship were much more complex than the problems in the symphony or sonata, and it was not until 1773—once again, the time of that musically catalytic visit to Vienna—that he ventured to attempt an original work in the form. He had earlier made seven rudimentary concertos by adding orchestral ritornellos and accompaniments to keyboard concertos by other composers, three [107] based on J. C. Bach sonatas, usually dated 1765 but possibly rather later, and four dating from 1767 [37, 39-41] on movements by Schobert and others.

It should not be imagined, however, that the form of a Mozart concerto is simply that of a sonata with ritornellos and accompaniments. The first movements are in fact very elaborate structures indeed. Basically their formal outlines are like those of ordinary sonata form, with an exposition (ending in the dominant key), a development and a recapitulation. But in a detailed analysis every one of the mature concertos turns out to be different; a formal scheme drawn up from one simply will not fit the workings of any other. Speaking in very general terms, they are mostly constructed along the following lines: first an orchestral ritornello, presenting at least two main themes, nearly always both in the tonic; then the solo entry, often starting with the material which opened the movement, followed (probably after a very brief ritornello and a modulation to the dominant) by the soloist's statement

Mozart's violin

of the second main theme and a new theme, the latter usually remaining his own exclusive property; then a ritornello followed by some kind of development, with opportunities for bravura and without a great deal of 'working-out'; and finally a recapitulation, back in the home key, with a cadenza near the end.

In Mozart's concertos, as in all other instrumental works of the period, the first movement was the weightiest and most substantial part. Once its complexities were done, relaxation was possible; Mozart could indulge his whim and allow the nature of his material to dictate the type of musical design. There are slow movements in binary, ternary, rondo, sonata and variation forms, while most of the finales have some kind of rondo structure—for the rondo is one of the easiest forms to take in and is consequently the most suitable to end a work, when the listener is beginning to tire.

Before looking at Mozart's concertos individually one further point should be made. Today the term 'virtuoso concerto' is commonly used in a derogatory sense, when applied to such composers as Liszt or Rachmaninov. Mozart's concertos, and Bach's too, are virtuoso concertos in that they are specifically designed to give the soloist an opportunity to shine—not by sheer weight or sheer velocity, which were not much appreciated for their own sakes in the temperate eighteenth century, but for such virtues as brilliance and evenness of touch, and above all taste and expressiveness. It was primarily for his expressive playing that Mozart himself was considered a great pianist.

Mozart's first wholly original effort in concerto form was the Concertone [190] (the title simply means a rather grand concerto) for two violins, oboe, cello and orchestra. Deeply indebted to J. C. Bach, who wrote many such multiple concertos, and to some extent to Michael Haydn, it is an expansive work full of grace and refinement, close to the serenade style. Mozart thought well enough of the Concertone to revive it in later years, notably at Mannheim, the home of the sinfonia concertante form, where his friends assured him it was 'just the thing for Paris'. A less lovable but much more significant work is the first of the piano concertos, K.175 in D, yet another consequence in all likelihood of that 1773 Viennese journey. While the texture and form of the bustling first movement offer only a glimpse of what Mozart was later to achieve, they are extraordinarily elaborate and inventive, especially considering the relative simplicity of the models available to him at the time—J. C. Bach and Wagenseil, and perhaps Dittersdorf, Vanhal, Haydn and C. P. E. Bach. This work too Mozart revived, with great success, in his Viennese days, dropping the not particularly entertaining original finale (which has passages of canonic texture) in favour of the pretty Rondo in D [382] of 1782, actually a set of variations despite its title.

Apart from the bassoon Concerto [191], a charming piece written most resourcefully for an awkward solo instrument, Mozart next concentrated on the violin concerto, in the concertante movements of his serenades and in a series of five works dating from 1775. The two earliest of these [207 and 211] show him slightly ill at ease with the form. No proper reconciliation is achieved between musical content and display, in the first movements especially; that of K.211 has a slightly old-fashioned early galant feeling, similar to the concertos by Nardini and other Italian virtuoso-composers Mozart had encountered.

An enormous and incomprehensible gulf separates these two concertos, written in the spring and early summer of 1775, from the three masterpieces composed between September and the end of the year. The sudden advance in Mozart's handling of the soloist-orchestra relationship can be seen in dozens of ways—the neat management of the first solo entry in the Concerto in G [216] is a good example (some of this material, incidentally, comes from an aria in Il rè pastore)—and this naturally led to his invention having freer rein. K.218 in D is modelled to some extent on a violin concerto probably by Boccherini; the one in A [219] is the most masterly, with a short, poetic Adagio at the first solo entry, followed by a sweeping new theme for the soloist appearing against the opening ritornello theme on the orchestra. All three concertos have slow movements of exquisite melodic beauty and rondo finales of a dance-like character, combining a French sense of elegance with more popular elements in the episodes—K.218 includes a musette connected with Strasburg and K.219 a Turkish section, partly culled from the ballet music for *Lucio Silla*, written two years earlier. These five are the only Mozart violin concertos of certain authenticity. No sensitive music-lover can accept K.268 or K.271a as pure Mozart, though there may be traces of his work in them somewhere.

Four more concertos, all for keyboard, date from the years preceding the journey to Paris. One [238] was written for Countess Lodron, another [246] for Countess Lützow, while the three-piano Concerto [242] was designed for Countess Lodron and her two daughters (one of them of slender ability, as the parts show). In these three works the spirit of the galant is extremely strong, and there is something of the elegance of the violin concertos about the *menuet en rondeau* finales of K.242 and 246. The last of the group, K.271 in E flat, written for a Mlle. Jeunehomme, is a very different matter: it marks a crucial stage in Mozart's use of the form and is justifiably the earliest of his piano concertos to have a firm place in the repertory.

K.271 proclaims its independence in its second bar, when the piano enters to answer the orchestra's opening phrase. In fact, this radical departure does not affect the music's form, for the indiscretion is quickly hushed up and the ritornello resumes its normal course. But the entry proper is scarcely less unconventional: the piano comes in with a long, high trill while the orchestra is still playing and then has an eloquent little four-bar solo before the opening material returns. Formally the movement is quite simple, with no extra material exclusive to the soloist, but there is a real development section, and to balance the opening the soloist intervenes in the closing ritornello. No less remarkable are the other movements—the sombre and deeply introspective Andantino in C minor, probably the longest of all his concerto slow movements and certainly his most personal movement of any kind to date, and the breathless Presto finale, which has as an interlude a very galant slow minuet with a highly ornamented variation.

Mozart's next concertos are much lighter in style, though not inferior, for on their less ambitious scale the three concertos written at Mannheim and Paris, two for flute, one for flute and harp, are certainly no less perfect than K.271. One could hardly guess from them that Mozart particularly disliked the flute. The flute and harp Concerto [299], written in Paris, is full of sensuous grace and happy writing for the two instruments, especially in its gavotte-like finale. The flute Concerto in G [313] too has an attractive finale, a *menuet en rondeau* again; Mozart wrote an alternative slow movement [315] for this work. Its companion piece in D [314] was originally an oboe Concerto in C, but the two versions seem so ideally planned for their respective instruments that without external evidence it would be hard to say which came first.

The Sinfonia Concertante for oboe, clarinet, bassoon and horn [297b] is generally taken to be Mozart's later version of the work for flute, oboe, bassoon and horn written for the Concert Spirituel, but there is so much about it which is crude and unMozartean, and entirely unlike the other works written in Paris, that it is hard to credit its complete authenticity. One has only to compare the unsubtle, dully repetitive style here with the brilliant interplay and dialogue of parts in the two multiple concertos written on his return from Paris to see how Mozart really tackled the problems of the sinfonia concertante. In the easy-going two-piano Concerto [365] there is an abundance of gaiety and polished wit in the give and take of the two soloists. More serious matters are dealt with in the Sinfonia Concertante in E flat for violin and viola [364]. The necessity for equality between the instruments, and consequently for saying almost everything twice over, gave Mozart marvellous opportunities for finding phrases that could turn in two different directions, one suited to the bright tones of the violin, the other designed for the viola's darker hues. The C minor Andante is a close relative of the Andantino in K.271, though with greater warmth, deriving from the profound sighs of its melodies and the richness of its harmony.

We are now approaching the time of the great piano concertos, but before embarking on them the short series of horn concertos, which started about the same time, is worth a mention. The horn was a very limited instrument in Mozart's day, capable of playing little more than the notes of the harmonic series, and Mozart was writing for his slightly buffoonish friend, Leutgeb; so naturally these four works do not demand to be taken over-seriously. To some extent they are modelled on the horn concertos of Rosetti, but Mozart far surpasses his model in the gay swing of his 'hunting' finales and the melodic interest he achieves with such limited means, especially in the slow movements. No. 3 [447] is perhaps the outstanding one.

The Viennese piano concertos start with the three Mozart wrote in 1782 for publication and for performance at his concerts. He described their style himself in a letter to his father:

'These concertos are a happy medium between what is too easy and too difficult; they are very brilliant, pleasing to the ear, and natural, without being vapid. There are passages here and there from which connoisseurs alone can derive satisfaction; but these passages are written in such a way that the less learned cannot fail to be pleased, though without knowing why.'

They were designed to be usable as chamber concertos, for piano and string quartet, a type of work very popular at the time (Mozart had in mind the published concertos of J. C. Bach and J. S. Schroeter). Consequently the wind parts are not of much significance. K.413 in F has no great distinction about its first two movements, but its J. C. Bach-like minuet finale is very charming. The formal C major mood appears in

From the title-page of the first edition of the piano concertos K.413-5

K.415, which has a brilliant and rather stiffly military first movement; here too the finale is of special interest, partly for its two brief Adagio episodes, the material of which Mozart rescued from an abandoned draft for the slow movement. K.414 in A is easily superior to its fellows, for its nice balance between virtuosity and musical interest and for its melodic grace and docility. In the first movement there is a good example of the 'interlude' type of development section—clearly Mozart was averting any possible suspicion of earnestness. The Andante, opening with the J. C. Bach echo mentioned on p. 80, is much more genuinely expressive, but in a more artificial, elegant manner than the slow movements of K.271 or 364. Mozart's original finale was a Rondo [386], which he rejected in favour of a gaily tripping Allegretto.

After a short break, Mozart came back to the piano concerto with a vengeance early in 1784, producing eight more in just over a year. Four of them were completed in about three months. Mozart sent copies home asking which of those in B flat, D and G his father and sister preferred. The one in E flat [449], he said, was of 'a quite peculiar kind', in that it could be played with only string accompaniment (like K.413-5).

It is much less spectacular than the others but no less attractive, deriving a special intimate flavour from its own particular blend of chamber-music atmosphere and concerto style. After a triple-time first movement full of serenely flowing melodic ideas, the Andantino opens with a gentle theme on the strings which provides a starting-point for florid piano arabesques, while its dreamy second subject (below) looks

ahead to the atmosphere of *Figaro* or even *Così*. But the concerto's glory is its finale. The semi-contrapuntal settings of the buoyant main theme are not to be taken too seriously: Mozart is not being 'learned' here but is merely bringing in a few ingenious contrapuntal tricks to enliven and enrich this bubbling movement.

'I regard them both as concertos to make the performer sweat', Mozart wrote of the pair in B flat and D [450-1]. The latter is thematically rather dull, and has much of the conventional D major manner; but its formal strength makes it a broadly satisfying work. The B flat, despite its technical difficulties, has room for melodic freshness and grace, and is the first of the concertos with the rich woodwind writing which lends the mature ones their special colour. The Andante is a deeply tender set of variations and the finale a vivacious 6/8 'hunting' movement.

Variations appear again in the next two concertos. K.453 in G—like K.449, written for Mozart's pupil Barbara Ployer, and likewise slightly feminine in character compared with the concertos 'to make the performer sweat'—has a warmly elegant first movement, an Andante mostly calm and contemplative but with a latent passion which sometimes disturbs the smooth surface, and a final set of variations on a perky, whistle-able Allegretto tune which is said to have been suggested to Mozart by a starling. The variations in K.456 in B flat form the slow movement. Their key, G minor, leads one to expect great things, though in fact this is a movement more of sensibility than of depth—there is slightly too artificial an air about it. But it is graced by some marvellous writing for the flute, oboes and bassoons. The use of woodwind is a feature of this concerto: in the first movement, where some sinister *sforzandos* and chromaticisms introduce a darker note into the innocent freshness typical of Mozart's B flat music, there is a theme in dialogue where the woodwind almost seem to be taking the parts of Figaro, Susanna and the Countess. The finale is very like that of K.450, but a trifle less irresistible; during a strange episode in the remote regions of B minor the piano, then the woodwind, play in 2/4 time against the prevailing 6/8.

K.459 in F begins with a favourite rhythm—  —common to the openings of K.415, 451, 453 and 456. Here it dictates more than usual of the work's character, which is open-air and military. Perhaps the finale, a high-spirited romp despite its fugatos, is the work's finest movement. Once again there is rich and elaborate interplay between woodwind and piano.

The D minor [466] marks a departure from the previous style of concerto, as its opening bars show:

With its sombre, passionate colouring and its more subjective character, this concerto has all the seeds of the Beethovenian and the romantic piano concerto. The slow movement is a Romanza in rondo form, with a fiery second episode acting as an antidote to the languor of the perhaps too artfully innocent main theme. In the finale the first movement's storms and stresses are revived, but they clear, and the ending is cheerful, at least on the surface.

No less great is the D minor's companion piece, in C [467], a symphonic work of immense breadth and grandeur. Its Andante is unique— a cantilena of miraculous beauty against an accompaniment of throbbing triplets, pizzicato basses and sustaining or intervening woodwind, with a harmonic background so richly chromatic and complex that Leopold could write of it:

'Several passages simply do not harmonise unless one hears all the instruments playing together. But of course it is quite possible that the copyist may have read a sharp for a flat in the score or something of the kind . . .'

The next three concertos are products of the months during which Mozart worked on *Figaro*. They are the only ones calling for clarinets. In the E flat [482] he was obviously revelling in the smooth, sensuous beauty of sound of the wind ensemble. Twice the concerto wanders towards the realms of the wind serenade, in a slow minuet (shades of K.271) inserted in the 'hunting' finale, and in an episode in the C minor slow movement. The sombre opening of this Andante also recalls

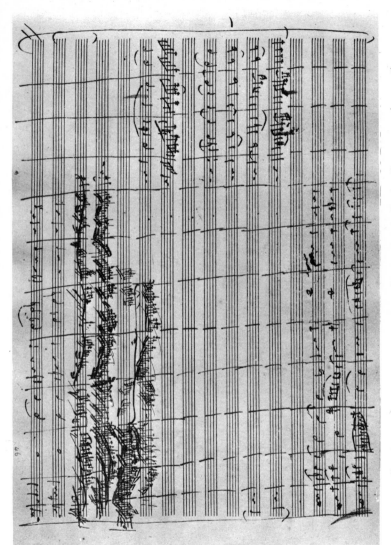

Manuscript of the Piano Concerto in C minor, K.491, showing Mozart's alterations (last movement, bars 37–48)

K.271, but the concentrated quality of the earlier movement is lacking here. In K.488, the popular A major Concerto, the trumpets and drums of K.482 are absent and a more intimate mood prevails. This is one of Mozart's most gently poetic and least overtly virtuoso concertos, with a siciliana-like slow movement in F sharp minor (his only use of the key) of a loveliness which is profoundly tranquil.

This group ends with the C minor [491], Mozart's second and last minor-key concerto. Its sinister, chromatic unison beginning suggests a work of passion like its predecessor, and there are other resemblances— the soloist has a special introductory theme of his own, for example, and the slow movement is again in Romanza style (but this one is superior, for the main theme cloys less and the woodwind episodes, with both oboes and clarinets, provide better variety). It is in fact a less dramatic work, less full of protest, though scarcely less powerful in impact. In the finale, a set of variations on a darkly coloured theme, the predominating sombre mood is relieved by two major-key variations, one in A flat and one in C, where a shaft of pale sunlight pierces the clouds. It does not threaten to disperse them, though, and despite the traditional change to a cheerful 6/8 rhythm for the last variation, the music's mood and key—and integrity—survive.

A view of the Augarten, Vienna; Mozart and his wife frequently walked in the avenues here and he gave concerts in the concert-room

With K.503 we are back in the world of C major pomp and spaciousness, and in the world of Mozartean counterpoint, for this first movement is one of those where contrapuntal processes play an important but well concealed part. For the last time, there is an introduction for the soloist: obviously one is needed, for a pianistic paraphrase of the grandiose orchestral opening could only sound absurd. Instead, the soloist is gently ushered in and has a chance to cast off his apparent initial shyness before the orchestra bursts in with the opening material, which the soloist answers in the only possible way, *con bravura*. The slow movement is full of beautiful detail, with rich woodwind writing, looking ahead to the *Jupiter* slow movement.

After the glories of the last dozen concertos, the relative weakness of the *Coronation*, in D [537], comes as a surprise. It was written under stress, and evidently in too much haste for the left-hand part to be completed. Even so, the concessions to virtuosity and the poverty of melodic and textural interest are disappointing. In the last piano concerto, in B flat [595], there is no such falling-off. Music full of serene resignation, it can all too easily be seen as a farewell, with its sense of fully spent passion and willing acceptance of the inevitable. The utter simplicity of the Larghetto—simplicity which is, of course, deceptive— has about it a negative quality, as if drained of earthly emotion. In the first movement too, especially in the chromatic distortions of the opening theme, there is something of the same feeling.

Only the clarinet Concerto [622] was to follow; it was Mozart's last instrumental work. Warmer than the death-chilled K.595, it recalls two other works in the same key, A major, the piano Concerto K.488 in its first movement and the clarinet Quintet in its Adagio. Mozart's relish of the clarinet's sound is apparent in every bar, and a work so full of affection makes an appropriate ending to this great and uniquely personal series.

Lorenzo da Ponte (engraving by Pekenino after Rogers)

The Operas

It was not simply because success in the opera house meant worldly success that opera was the form which mattered most of all to Mozart. Unlike many composers, among them Haydn and Schubert, Mozart had a real sense of the theatre. He also had a penetrating insight into the vagaries of human character, shown time and again in his letters. It is these gifts, allied to his purely musical genius, which give his operas their special place as the quintessential part of his art.

But it would be an over-simplification, and very unfair to Mozart, to mention this blend of gifts without outlining the background circumstances which militated so potently against them. Mozart's operas were mostly created under what a present-day composer would consider appalling artistic handicaps. To have to plan each part round the personality and capabilities of a particular singer—and rewrite it all if the singer disliked it; to have to deal with impossible plots, unreal situations and lifeless characters; to have to include, very often, an *aria di licenza*, usually irrelevant to the story, in praise of the local potentate; and to have to write for an audience which only half attended to the stage while talking, supping, playing cards or flirting: these were the normal circumstances under which an eighteenth-century opera composer worked, and which he did not think to question.

It was only through Mozart's supreme artistic sensibility that, with the help of a brilliant librettist, he eventually managed to rise above these conditions. But it is worth remembering that he was a man of his time right to the end of his life. While in the actual act of creating one of his great operas, the work, as an artistic entity, dominated everything; but when adapting the same work for later revivals he considered only

In the Alte Residenztheater, Munich (where 'Idomeneo' was first performed), at its re-opening in 1958.

expediency, adding music which utterly shattered the dramatic flow and the integrity of the characterisation.

It is primarily on account of the conditions governing eighteenth-century opera that none of Mozart's operas prior to *Idomeneo* [366] can ever be appreciated in stage performance without the making of a colossal historical effort. From this time onwards Mozart had sufficient discrimination and a sufficiently developed dramatic sense to turn down an unsuitable libretto or to modify an acceptable one. This is not, of course, to say that the music of the earliest operas should be forgotten. There is much of charm in works as early as *La finta semplice* or the little one-act German opera *Bastien und Bastienne*, and by the time of *La finta giardiniera* and *Il rè pastore* one can find the beginnings of real musical characterisation and something as near to dramatic life as the librettos—in one case rather childishly comic, in the other stiff and old-fashioned—allow.

We have already seen that Mozart, from the time of the Paris visit onwards, was anxious to find an opportunity to write an opera. The 1780 Munich commission gave him his opportunity. It was no doubt convenient to have a local Salzburg man as his librettist for *Idomeneo*, but Mozart must eventually have felt the advantages to be offset by Abbé Varesco's obstinacy, pompousness and lack of any kind of dramatic feeling. Mozart naturally wrote most of the music in Munich; as he worked on it he saw again and again the necessity for modifications in the libretto—nearly all of them cuts, for Varesco, still wedded to the old Metastasian concepts of *opera seria*, planned to end each scene with an 'exit aria', so vitiating the continuity of the action. It is clear from Mozart's letters home (he communicated with Varesco through his father) that he had been much influenced by the more dramatic and up-to-date operas he had seen in Paris—not Gluck's operas, for neither Mozart himself nor the Munich singers would have wanted the normal division between *secco* recitatives and formal set-piece arias to be ironed out, but of the type represented by Piccini. This applies most of all to his liberal use of the chorus, which rarely appears in Italian operas; only in his dramatic use of accompanied recitative does Mozart follow Gluck. The oracle scene in *Alceste* may have been the model for his 'subterranean voice', but this was the obvious way to set such a passage, and in any case Mozart was partly following his father's suggestions.

As to the music itself, there is nothing else quite like it in all Mozart's output. *Idomeneo* is an *opera seria*, not *buffa* like Mozart's later Italian operas, and the heroic, exalted nature of the subject drew from him music on a consistently high level of invention. The equally consistent

A scene from 'Idomeneo'

intensity of expression is possibly a weakness, not so much a weakness of Mozart's as one potentially inherent in the form itself (and one which scarcely mattered when audiences did not concentrate). Mozart's musical characterisation is impaired by the stiffness of the mythological figures. Only the jealous spitfire Electra really emerges with much of a personality, and that, as shown in her Act I vengeance aria and her madness aria in Act III, is not entirely consistent with the calm contemplation of happiness in her Act II aria. As a whole, the music is among Mozart's richest, but the opera is so long and on so intense a level that it is apt to leave one with a touch of musical indigestion.

The Seraglio [384] is a very different matter. It is a Singspiel, a light opera in German with spoken dialogue rather than recitative. The plot is extremely simple: it concerns the attempted elopement of Constanze, a prisoner in the Pasha Selim's harem (of which she is not, despite all efforts at persuasion, what might be called an active member), with her lover Belmonte. They are, of course, recaptured, but spared and freed by the unnaturally magnanimous Pasha. This was a standard type of plot in the eighteenth century, with its overtones of praise for generous and enlightened monarchs. As subsidiary characters there are the lovers' two servants, forming a secondary pair of lovers, and the Pasha's lecherous servant Osmin. The plot is very similar to that of the incomplete Singspiel *Zaïde* which Mozart had worked on during 1779 and which can be seen as a kind of sketch for, or stepping-stone towards, *The Seraglio*.

During the autumn of 1781 Mozart wrote a number of letters to Leopold telling him how the composition of *The Seraglio* was progressing. The letters of the 26th of September and the 13th of October are well worth reading for anyone who wants to understand Mozart's operatic aesthetic. Not that he really had an operatic aesthetic, as such: rather, he had a powerful instinct for what was practical and effective in the theatre, together with complete conviction of the dramatic and expressive power of music. When he wrote, in the second of these letters, that 'the poetry must be altogether the obedient daughter of the music' he should certainly not be taken as contradicting Gluckist (or Wagnerian) principles. In the last resort, Gluck's and Wagner's operas live on account of their music; Mozart, with his sure instinct, arrived at a truth which Gluck and Wagner, with their rigorous intellectual approach, could never reach—that ultimately an opera stands or falls not by the literary merit of the libretto, nor even wholly by the quality of the music, but by whether the libretto has the right qualities (partly negative ones) to give the composer the musical freedom and scope he needs, and by whether the composer knows how to use this freedom. Mozart did know.

But even so *The Seraglio* is not a complete success. For one thing, most of the numbers are far too long: Stephanie's concept of a play with songs meant that the songs were nearly all static, dramatically

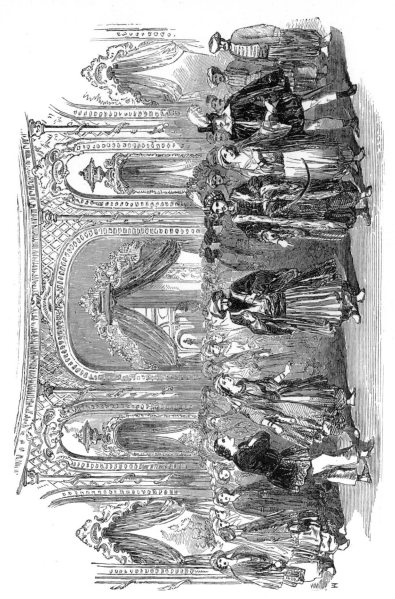

A scene from 'The Seraglio' (a nineteenth-century production at Drury Lane Theatre, London)

speaking; and that meant that they ought to be short. Facing similar problems in *The Magic Flute* ten years later, Mozart did not make this mistake. He admitted that he sacrificed Constanze's first aria a little to the 'flexible throat' of Mlle. Cavalieri. But her third aria shows still greater sacrifice, the famous and magnificent 'Martern aller Arten'. It is entirely out of place here, as Mozart must have realised, not only because it immediately follows her pathetic G minor lament but also on account of its enormous scale: the long introduction, with four obbligato instruments, completely kills the effect of her defiant flinging of the Pasha's words, 'All kinds of torture', back in his face.

There is much else in *The Seraglio* which has to be mentioned—Belmonte's tenderness, the sprightliness of Constanze's English maid, Blonde, and the semi-comic savagery of Osmin (perfectly drawn in his final aria, 'Ha! wie will ich triumphieren'). The Janissary choruses, with their Turkish colouring, are another happy idea. One of the finest movements is the quartet ending Act II, where the lovers are reunited and plan to escape. The two men, however, have sneaking doubts as to the women's fidelity: at the same time Mozart manages to convey Blonde's spirited reaction—a smart slap on Pedrillo's face—and Constanze's real distress at Belmonte's suspicion.

A view of St. Michael's Square, Vienna; in the right foreground is the Burgtheater, where 'The Seraglio', 'The Marriage of Figaro' and Così fan tutte' were first performed

Four members of the original cast of 'Figaro': top left, Paolo Stefano Mandini, the Count; top right, Luisa Laschi–Mombelli, the Countess; bottom left, Dorothea Bussani, the Cherubino; bottom right, Michael Kelly, the Basilio and Curzio

Never Acted.

Theatre Royal, Covent-Garden

This present SATURDAY, March 6, 1819,

Will be acted a Comick Opera, (in three acts) called The

Marriage of Figaro

[Founded on BEAUMARCHAIS's Comedy 'La Folle Journée,' & on 'the Follies of a Day.']

The OVERTURE and MUSICK selected chiefly from MOZART's Operas.

The new Musick composed, & the whole arranged & adapted to the English Stage, by *Mr. BISHOP*

The Scenery painted by Mess. Phillips, Whitmore, Pugh, Grieve and Sons.
The Dresses by Mr. Palmer and Miss Egan.

Count Almaviva by Mr. JONES,
Fiorello by Mr. DURUSET,
Figaro by Mr. LISTON,
Antonio *(the Gardener)* by Mr. FAWCETT,
Basil, Mr. J. ISAACS, Sebastian, Mr. COMER,
Cherubino *(the Page)* Miss BEAUMONT,

Countess Almaviva by Mrs. DICKONS,
Susanna by Miss STEPHENS,
Barbarina, Mrs. LISTON, Marcellina, Mrs. STERLING,

In act III.

A SPANISH FESTIVAL,

In which will be introduced
A PAS DE DEUX by Mr. NOBLE, and Miss LUPPINO,

The Villagers by
Mesdames Chipp, Louis, Mori, Newton, Robinson, Twamley, Vedy, Wells.
Mess. Collet, Goodwin, Gouriet, Grant, Heath, Louis, Platt, Vedy
The Dances composed by Mr. NOBLE.

The CHORUSES by

Mess. Crumpton, Everard, George, Guichard, Healy, Lee, Montague, Norris, G. Pyne,
I. S. & C. Tett, Watson, Williams
Mesds. Appleton, Baggs, Bologna, Chipp, Coates, Corri, Green, Grimaldi, Healy, Herbert, Hibbert,
Iliff, Norman, Parrin, Port, Sexton, Shaw, Smith, Tokely, Watts, Whitmore, Wood.

Playbill of the first production of 'Figaro' at Covent Garden

No complete operas followed until *The Marriage of Figaro* [492], four years later. In the meantime Mozart started setting two other librettos, *L'oca del Cairo* and *Lo sposo deluso* (and perhaps a third, *Il regno delle Amazoni*), but abandoned them, presumably when he realised how unsatisfactory they were. This if nothing else gives the lie to Wagner's ill-informed observation that Mozart set 'any and every operatic text offered him.' Just before *Figaro* he wrote *The Impresario*, which, although an insignificant trifle, at least dealt with real human beings of a kind with which Mozart was familiar—all too familiar—for it concerned the claims of two rival sopranos upon an impresario.

During the years following *The Seraglio*, when he was looking for a libretto, Mozart made the acquaintance of several *opere buffe* with texts by such accomplished poets as Casti and Bertati, far superior in construction and sense of character to anything he had come across before. Then he met da Ponte. The two probably decided together that Beaumarchais' *Le Mariage de Figaro* could be adapted as an opera, with some pruning of the characters and sufficient blunting of the political points (which had caused the original to be banned at first in Paris) to make it acceptable to the Viennese authorities.

If some particular element of *Figaro* has to be chosen for discussion it should perhaps be the ensembles—though it is impossible to pass over such gems among the arias as Cherubino's 'Non so più', the perfect evocation of adolescent love, or Susanna's 'Deh vieni', where she is singing with sincerity about her approaching bliss but allowing Figaro to believe her bliss is to be with the Count, or Figaro's aria immediately before, when he thinks himself deceived and sings with ironic humour of women's ways (a really serious aria would be out of character). One could go on indefinitely. But the arias are naturally more static dramatically than the ensembles, in which the opera is especially rich. Susanna, who is really the key character, takes part in all of them. In Act I she sings in three duets, two with Figaro and one with Marcellina, which give us a clearly etched picture of her character—lively, a trifle coquettish, but entirely faithful to Figaro. The principal ensemble in this act is the trio for Susanna, the Count and Basilio, when the Count discovers Cherubino in hiding; Susanna's confusion, the Count's anger and Basilio's relish of the situation are marvellously portrayed in the music.

For musical portrayal of situation, however, the Act II finale stands supreme. Starting with the Count's entry and Cherubino's concealment, the tension rises as the Count swears vengeance on the ubiquitous page —only to find that it was Susanna hiding in the bedroom, whence she emerges to the demurest possible music. But the most nerve-tingling moment of all is when the Count is interrogating Figaro, first about a letter, then, to a naggingly persistent accompaniment, about the page's commission. At last all is safely negotiated, and the tensions resolved, when the entry of Marcellina and her fellow conspirators creates confusion once again.

I alone was a stickler for Mozart, and naturally enough, for he had a claim on my warmest wishes, from my adoration of his powerful genius, and the debt of gratitude I owed him, for many personal favours.

The mighty contest was put an end to by His Majesty issuing a mandate for Mozart's "Nozze di Figaro," to be instantly put into rehearsal; and none more than Michael O'Kelly, enjoyed the little great man's triumph over his rivals.

Of all the performers in this opera at that time, but one survives—myself. It was allowed that never was opera stronger cast. I have seen it performed at different periods in other countries, and well too, but no more to compare with its original performance than light is to darkness. All the original performers had the advantage of the instruction of the composer, who transfused into their minds his inspired meaning. I never shall forget his little animated countenance, when lighted up with the glowing rays of genius;—it is as impossible to describe it, as it would be to paint sun-beams.

I called on him one evening; he said to me, "I have just finished a little duet for my opera, you shall hear it." He sat down to the piano, and we sang it. I was delighted with it, and the musical world will give me credit for being so, when I mention the duet,

sung by Count Almaviva and Susan, "Crudel perchè finora farmi languire cosi." A more delicious morceau never was penned by man, and it has often been a source of pleasure to me, to have been the first who heard it, and to have sung it with its greatly gifted composer. I remember at the first rehearsal of the full band, Mozart was on the stage with his crimson pelisse and gold-laced cocked hat, giving the time of the music to the orchestra. Figaro's song, "Non più andrai, farfallone amoroso," Bennuci gave, with the greatest animation, and power of voice.

I was standing close to Mozart, who, sotto voce, was repeating, Bravo! Bravo! Bennuci; and when Bennuci came to the fine passage, "Cherubino, alla vittoria, alla gloria militar," which he gave out with Stentorian lungs, the effect was electricity itself, for the whole of the performers on the stage, and those in the orchestra, as if actuated by one feeling of delight, vociferated Bravo! Bravo! Maestro. Viva, viva, grande Mozart. Those in the orchestra I thought would never have ceased applauding, by beating the bows of their violins against the music desks. The little man acknowledged, by repeated obeisances, his thanks for the distinguished mark of enthusiastic applause bestowed upon him.

Their conspiring, however, comes to an end in the main Act III ensemble, the sextet where Figaro is discovered to be the son of Marcellina and Bartolo. Here Mozart again portrays different emotions simultaneously: the sentimental affection of reunited parents and son on the one hand, and the frustrated fury of the Count, in which he is joined by the lawyer, on the other—the angry dotted rhythms and chromaticisms of one group are set off by the docile rhythms and the very different, sentimental, chromaticisms of the other. When Susanna enters she is at first in the angry group, on seeing Figaro and Marcellina embracing, but joins the other when the position is explained to her.

The weakest part of the opera is the last act, where Mozart was obliged to insert arias for the two singers who had not yet had any, Marcellina and Basilio. In practice these pieces, which not surprisingly have little musical and only a negative dramatic value, are usually omitted. The finale is again full of subtle changes of pace and adjustments of tension. Through all the scenes of mistaken identity—with the Count making love to his own wife (of all unlikely things), then Figaro making love to Susanna while pretending to think she is the Countess, and then their deliberate re-enactment of the scene for the Count's benefit—the music provides a kind of commentary, with such a touch as the burlesque of operatic love-scene phrases when Figaro is making love tongue-in-cheek as an obvious example. The great climax, where the enraged Count repeatedly refuses to forgive his wife her apparent

The 'Champagne Aria' from 'Don Giovanni',
with Giuseppe Ambrogetti as Giovanni (1817)

infidelity, and then the real Countess emerges to add her voice to the pleas, is one of those unforgettable moments where comedy rises far above itself: we are lifted to a higher plane for a moment and given a glimpse of the ultimate tragedy of human relationships which lies behind the entire opera. The musical means are ridiculously simple, but it takes profound genius to find them.

Don Giovanni [527] was the fruit of Mozart and da Ponte's second collaboration. It was written in something of a rush and there was no time for the careful moulding *Figaro* had undergone. The plot was a traditional Italian pot-boiler existing in many different versions, including recent ones by Goldoni and Bertati on which da Ponte drew. It needed considerable expansion to make a full-length *opera buffa*, and the added material in the middle of the opera somewhat mars the dramatic coherence of the whole. All the first part of Act II is irrelevant temporising—but what temporising! Only a boor could object to undramatic episodes if they provide such music as that of the trio where Elvira softens as she believes Don Giovanni to be returning to her, or Don Giovanni's serenade, or Zerlina's 'Vedrai, carino', where she finally succeeds in pacifying Masetto both in body and soul.

The Act I finale is another insertion of da Ponte's, and a splendid one. It is less deliciously eventful than its equivalent in *Figaro* (the Act II finale) but is more striking in its cumulative dramatic effect, with its tremendous climax building up during the minuet (simultaneously with

Henriette Sontag (c. 1805-54) as Donna Anna in 'Don Giovanni'

Don Giovanni: the ballroom scene (*a nineteenth-century production at Her Majesty's Theatre, London*)

a waltz and a contradance) to the moment when Zerlina screams, off-stage, and Anna, Elvira and Ottavio unmask and confront Giovanni.

The singularly ineffectual and static character of Don Ottavio is one of the drama's weaknesses. He has aptly been described as a 'melodious nit-wit'. But otherwise the characterisation is superb. The three women in particular are finely differentiated by their music—Zerlina as a simple peasant girl, Anna as a proud, rather frigid and tragic figure, Elvira as warmer and more womanly, deeply mortified by Don·Giovanni's desertion and forced back on what dignity she has left ('Mi tradì' is a later addition and perhaps not wholly in character). None of them could sing music written for another without incongruity.

One cannot leave a discussion of *Don Giovanni* without mention of the 'comedy or tragedy' argument. Historically speaking, there can be no doubt that it is an *opera buffa*; Mozart and da Ponte used the conventional term '*dramma giocoso*', which means precisely the same. But *Don Giovanni* is hardly an *opera buffa* in the sense that such works as Paisiello's *Barber of Seville* or Cimarosa's *Secret Marriage*, or indeed Mozart's *Figaro*, are. No other *opera buffa* could yield a parallel to the great supper scene, the climax to the whole opera, with the terrifying descent of the still defiant Giovanni to eternal hellfire. Possibly this is Mozart's greatest single operatic scene. To present-day taste its impact may be blunted by the final sextet, but one has to remember that an eighteenth-century audience did not like to be sent away in a serious, chastened mood. (Mozart risked precisely that in the Viennese production, cutting the sextet simply because the opera was too long.) However, *Don Giovanni* is still further from the world of *opera seria*: clearly Giovanni himself could never be considered in terms of high drama, and in a different way the respective plights of Anna and Elvira would be unthinkable in such terms. One can only accept it as a unique *opera buffa*, where the composer was carried away by the nature of the subject into creating something which burst the bounds of the form.

Così fan tutte [588] was the third and last da Ponte-Mozart collaboration. The plot here is entirely original (or it may have been based on a real occurrence in Vienna) and the libretto is much the best designed of the three. In consequence the opera, in its less ambitious way, is even more perfect dramatically than *Figaro* or *Don Giovanni*. The cynical nature of the plot, with its debunking of feminine fidelity, has naturally drawn much censorious comment from nineteenth-century moralists, among them the creators of Leonora and Isolde. But one does not have to be a cynic to know that women, or men for that matter, do not infrequently succumb to the charms of a rival when the beloved is absent. Perhaps it is a little overwhelmingly immoral for it all to happen within a few hours, but da Ponte was anxious to observe the classical unities here (as in *Figaro* and *Don Giovanni*; it is equally unlikely that the Commandant's statue would have been erected within twenty-four hours of his death—the point being that one simply has to suspend all standards

'Don Giovanni': the ballroom scene (a Salzburg production)

of everyday life on entering the opera house, whatever 'realists' may aim at).

Yet Mozart and da Ponte did not really intend the plot of *Così* to be taken with complete seriousness. The characters behave as people do behave, but they are slightly larger than life size, and there is a strong element of parody. One is sometimes a little uncertain about the precise direction of the parody—in the famous 'Come scoglio', for example, where Fiordiligi determines to be as firm as a rock, is Mozart mocking at the conventional heroine's aria, or Fiordiligi's self-deception (for we know the rock is of sand), or both?

But there is no need to worry about the answer: the music of *Così* is so delectable, so fragrant and so tenderly sensuous that it can be enjoyed purely for its own sake. The distinction of character between the two women is beautifully managed. In Dorabella's music, except for her exaggeratedly passionate first aria, one can detect a touch of coquetry, while Fiordiligi is more of the stuff that tragic heroines are made of and surrenders less readily to the 'Albanian'. Her part, designed for da Ponte's current mistress, is the richer; as well as 'Come scoglio' there is the splendid rondo in E major, 'Per pietà', as she resists the unwelcome onset of love. This aria with two obbligato horns was surely Beethoven's model for Leonora's 'Abscheulicher!' in *Fidelio*. Perhaps the most exquisite moments come in two of the ensembles: the lovely, tearful farewell quintet in the first act (with Don Alfonso shaking with laughter in the background) and the garden scene in Act II—no mortal woman, unless she had a heart of stone, could resist a lover's pleadings after that marvellous serenade.

And thus Mozart bade farewell to *opera buffa*. His only other Italian opera, *La clemenza di Tito* [621], was an untimely reversion to Metastasian *opera seria*—untimely because this stiff, static form was totally unsuited to the mature Mozart's dramatic outlook and gifts. In his more prosperous days Mozart would surely have refused to touch a libretto by Metastasio, however skilfully modernised, but in 1791 he was in no position to refuse. The choice of the fifty-seven-year-old text was dictated by political considerations. In the anxious months following the French Revolution it was thought prudent, especially at coronation festivities, to emphasise the wisdom and generosity of monarchs—though Titus' clemency, like the Pasha Selim's, was more than anyone could reasonably believe in.

It is not true to say that *Titus* is musically weak, for it is full of beautiful music of superlative technical craftsmanship. The trouble is that the text effectively killed any possibility of producing a work with real human feeling or dramatic shape. There are two great concert-type arias with obbligato parts for Mozart's friend Stadler, one for clarinet and one for basset-horn, and the second of the two duets is very attractive. Otherwise the most effective scene is the Act I finale, where Rome is burning and there is a dramatic offstage chorus for the terrified populace.

Frontispiece of the first edition of the vocal score of 'La clemenza di Tito', depicting a scene from the opera

Finally we come to *Die Zauberflöte* (*The Magic Flute*) [620]. German critics, on account of its position in the Mozart canon, its 'seriousness' and its symbolic meanings, and of course its German language, have tended to assume that it must necessarily be the greatest of his operas. But the comparisons implied by such judgements are meaningless: it is hardly more than an accident of nomenclature that the sublime pantomime-cum-ritual which constitutes *The Magic Flute* should today be called by the same name as the earlier musico-dramatic masterpieces in Italian.

The origins of *The Magic Flute* and the symbolism which runs through it are of the utmost importance for its understanding. The libretto, by Schikaneder, is partly derived from a romance by Terrasson, *Sethos*. Most of the characters, all the initiation rites and even some of the text come from this book, which had a considerable vogue in eighteenth-century masonic circles. The characters also had a further symbolic meaning, with the Queen of Night representing the Empress Maria Theresa (an enemy of freemasonry), Sarastro representing the scientist and freemason Ignaz von Born, and so on. To Mozart and the intellectual circle to which he belonged the masonic significance was of the greatest consequence. He felt that he was on the side of freedom and enlightenment against oppression and ignorance, and by incorporating masonic ideas and even something akin to masonic ritual in *The Magic Flute* he was undoubtedly aiming to further the cause.

The masonic significance, it seems, had no part in the work's original scheme. At first it was to be a simple tale about a prince rescuing a fairy queen's beautiful daughter from the clutches of a wicked magician, with

Josefa Hofer, Mozart's sister-in-law and the first Queen of Night in 'The Magic Flute'

the help of a magic flute. Mozart, uncertain how to write a 'magic opera', started to model his score on that of *Oberon*, a fairy-tale opera by Wranitzky to a libretto by Giesecke, which Schikaneder had successfully staged in 1789. He even borrowed a few of its musical ideas. But for some reason, possibly connected with a rival production, Mozart and his librettist decided to interchange the forces of good and evil; the deeper meaning was added and the symbolism took shape. No doubt Mozart's increasing interest in the work as he proceeded with its composition is closely related to its gradual transformation from a childish fairy-tale to a profound allegory.

It will be appreciated that the work's very nature precludes the kind of musical characterisation seen in the da Ponte operas. The characters in *The Magic Flute* are not ordinary human beings. Tamino is the personification of the ideal man and Pamina of the ideal woman, both of them undergoing severe ordeals before they can be united. They have no love scene—their love is taken for granted throughout—and only a single aria each, Tamino's famous 'Portrait aria' and Pamina's mournful 'Ach, ich fühl's', in G minor, when she believes Tamino has rejected her. Yet over the whole opera their music gives a marvellous sense of their gradual maturing into complete, though idealised, people.

Papageno's main function is to provide comic relief, to give the audiences something they could understand and laugh at. There is a world of difference between the slightly coarse Germanic humour in his arias, designed for the middle-class Viennese who patronised a suburban theatre, and the more sophisticated *buffo* arias in Mozart's Italian operas. The Queen of Night is of course the embodiment of the forces of evil—the coloratura of her second aria has a truly diabolical quality— while Sarastro stands at the opposite pole, with reason and wisdom permeating every note he sings. His spirit dominates all the music connected with the temple and the initiation rites, including the solemn and strange scene where Tamino and Pamina undergo the ordeals of fire and water. Finally, the music of the three ladies and the three boys: the simplicity and translucency of their three-part writing provides some of the score's most enchanting moments, especially the trio in the middle of Act II, with its tripping violins and the delicate colouring of the flutes and bassoons. If *The Magic Flute* cannot provide as brilliant an evening's entertainment as Mozart's three great Italian operas, it has something else to offer—a serene, almost religious quality, which leaves one spiritually richer and wiser.

It would be easy to end by saying that *The Magic Flute* summarises Mozart's musical achievement and his outlook on life. But this would be less than a half-truth. It may serve to show his philosophical outlook during his final months, which it does far more accurately than the Requiem. But there is no single work which in any sense epitomises his achievement. With composers like Bach or Handel, Haydn or Beethoven, Verdi or Wagner, such a work might be found, for these men had a clearer sense of purpose and long enough lives to see it fulfilled.

If there is no single climactic point to Mozart's output, but a whole range of peaks, this in itself emphasises the diversity of his achievement. The fact that he was equally accomplished in the vocal and instrumental fields, and that his style is a cosmopolitan mixture owing no special national allegiance, emphasises it further. Glancing back over Mozart's work, we see not only the achievement of the most naturally gifted of all composers but also that of the most universal artist who ever expressed himself through the medium of music.

Appendices

Papageno, the bird-catcher in 'The Magic Flute' (from the first edition of the libretto)

Chronology

MOZART		THE OTHERS
1756	Wolfgang Amadeus Mozart born at Salzburg, 27th January, son of Leopold Mozart (37).	Abel 31, Adlgasser 28, Anfossi 29, Arne 46, Bach (W. F.) 46, Bach (C. P. E.) 42, Bach (J. C.) 21, Benda (F.) 47, Benda (G.) 34, Boccherini 14, Boyce 46, Cannabich 25, Cimarosa 7, Clementi 4, Dittersdorf 17, Eberlin 54, Galuppi 50, Gassmann 36, Geminiani 69, Gluck 42, Gossec 22, Grétry 14, Guglielmi 29, Handel 71, Hasse 57, Haydn (F. J.) 24, Haydn (J. M.) 19, Hiller 28, Holzbauer 45, Hook 10, Jommelli 42, Kozeluch 4, Locatelli 63, Martin y Soler 2, Martini 50, Monn *c.* 39, Monsigny 27, Mysliveček 19, Paisiello 16, Piccini 28, Porpora 70, Rameau 73, Richter 47, Sacchini 26, Salieri 6, Sammartini (G. B.) 55, Sarti 27, Scarlatti (D.) 71, Schobert *c.* 36, Stamitz (J. W. A.) 39, Stamitz (C.) 10, Tartini 64, Telemann 75, Vanhal 17, Viotti 3, Wagenseil 41.
1757		Scarlatti (D.) and Stamitz (J. W. A.) die, Pleyel born.
1759		Handel dies.
1760		Cherubini born.

	MOZART	THE OTHERS
1761		Dussek born.
1762	January–February, journey to Munich; September, journey to Vienna, staying there rest of year.	Eberlin and Geminiani die.
1763	January, return to Salzburg; June, beginning of 'grand tour', giving concerts—Munich, Augsburg, Ludwigsburg, Schwetzingen, Mainz, Frankfurt, Brussels, Paris (November).	Méhul and Storace born.
1764	In Paris until April; then London, meeting J. C. Bach, staying there rest of year.	Locatelli and Rameau die.
1765	In London until July; then to The Hague (delays due to illness)	
1766	Amsterdam and The Hague; then to Paris (May to July), returning through Lyons, Geneva, Zürich, Donaueschingen and Munich, arriving at Salzburg in November.	Süssmayr born.
1767	September, visit to Vienna, moving to Olomouc (attack of smallpox).	Porpora and Telemann die.
1768	January, return to Vienna; *La finta semplice* composed but not performed; *Bastien und Bastienne* composed and performed privately.	
1769	January, return to Salzburg; December, departure on first Italian journey— Rovereto, Verona.	
1770	January, on to Mantua and Milan; then Parma, Bologna, Florence (end of March) and Rome (April); May, visit to Naples; then back to Rome, receiving Order of Golden Spur from the Pope; July, to Bologna, studying under Martini, elected member of Accademia Filarmonica. October, return to Milan, to work on opera *Mitridate*, successfully produced 26th December.	Tartini dies, Beethoven born.
1771	Visits to Turin and Venice, then return to Salzburg via Padua, Vicenza, Verona. In Salzburg, end of March to mid-August; then departure for Milan for production of *Ascanio in Alba* at royal wedding festivities (17th October). Return to Salzburg, December.	
1772	Colloredo elected Archbishop of Salzburg, *Il sogno di Scipione* written for his installation. August, appointed konzertmeister at Salzburg court. Third journey to Italy, late October, for production of *Lucio Silla* in Milan (26th December).	

	MOZART	THE OTHERS
1773	Return to Salzburg, March. Visit to Vienna, mid-July to early October.	
1774	In Salzburg until December, then departure for Munich.	Gassmann and Jommelli die, Spontini born.
1775	*La finta giardiniera* produced at Munich, 13th January; return to Salzburg, early March; *Il rè pastore* produced there, 23rd April.	Sammartini (G. B.) dies, Boieldieu born.
1776	Whole year spent in Salzburg.	
1777	In Salzburg until August; then, resigning court post, departure with mother for Munich, Augsburg and Mannheim (end of October).	Adlgasser and Wagenseil die.
1778	Friendship with Mannheim composers, falls in love with Aloysia Weber. Unable to obtain appointment at Mannheim, goes to Paris (mid-March); refuses organist's post at Versailles, has works performed at Concert Spirituel, meets J. C. Bach again. His mother dies, 3rd July. With no prospects in Paris, leaves for home (September), via Strasburg, Mannheim and Munich.	Arne dies, Hummel born.
1779	Arrives back in Salzburg, mid-January, to take up appointment under better terms than previously; spends rest of year there.	Boyce dies.
1780	In Salzburg until early November, then departure for Munich, to complete opera for production there.	
1781	*Idomeneo* produced at Munich (29th January). Summoned to join Archbishop's entourage in Vienna, mid-March; crisis in relations with Archbishop, culminating in complete break in May. Stays with Weber family, becoming friendly with Constanze and promising to marry her. Appears at Viennese court, meets Haydn.	Mysliveček dies.
1782	Becoming established in Viennese musical life, giving concerts, taking pupils etc. *The Seraglio* produced (16th July). Marriage to Constanze Weber, 4th August.	Bach (J. C.) dies, Auber and Field born.
1783	Visit to Salzburg, July–October, returning to Vienna via Linz.	Hasse and Holzbauer die.
1784	Continuing successfully to establish himself as a leading composer, pianist and teacher in Vienna. Becomes a freemason.	Bach (W. F.) and Martini die, Spohr born.

	MOZART	THE OTHERS
1785	Friendship with Haydn continues; meets da Ponte, starts collaboration with him on *The Marriage of Figaro*. Leopold Mozart visits his son in Vienna.	Galuppi dies.
1786	*The Impresario* produced at Schönbrunn (7th February); *Figaro* produced (1st May).	Benda (F.) and Sacchini die, Weber born.
1787	Visit to Prague, January; return visit in September, for production of *Don Giovanni* (29th October); on return to Vienna, mid-November, appointed court chamber musician by Joseph II, in place of Gluck. Leopold Mozart dies, 28th May.	Gluck dies.
1788	*Don Giovanni* given in Vienna (7th May); financial difficulties worsen, and general standing in Vienna's musical life declines.	Bach (C. P. E.) dies.
1789	Early April, departure with Prince Lichnowsky for Berlin, via Dresden, Leipzig (playing at St. Thomas's); meets Friedrich Wilhelm II at Potsdam, accepts commission from him; returns to Vienna, via Dresden and Prague. Constanze ill, takes cure at Baden.	Richter dies.
1790	*Così fan tutte* produced (26th January); late September, visit to Frankfurt during coronation festivities, returning via Mainz, Mannheim and Munich. Constanze again ill. Financial situation worsens.	
1791	Constanze again ill in summer and away at Baden. Composes *Magic Flute* during summer; accepts commissions for a Requiem and an opera, *La clemenza di Tito*, for Prague. Departure for Prague for its production (6th September). Returns to Vienna, mid-September, in failing health. *Magic Flute* produced (30th September). Illness becomes more acute, prevents completion of Requiem; dies 1 a.m., 5th December.	Czerny, Hérold and Meyerbeer born.

List of Works

SACRED MUSIC

(a) MASSES

G, 49 (47d)
d, 65 (61a)
C, 66 (Dominicus)
c, 139 (114a)
C, 115 (166d)*
C, 167
F, 192 (186f)
D, 194 (186h)
C, 220 (196b)
C, 262 (246a)
C, 257 (Credo)
C, 258
C, 259 (Organ Solo)
Bb, 275 (272b)
C, 317 (Coronation)
C, 337
c, 427 (417a)*
d, 626 (Requiem)*

(c) VESPERS

C, 321
C, 339

(d) KYRIES

F, 33
G, 89 (73k)
d, 90
C, 93b (221)
Eb, 322 (296a)
C, 323*
d, 341 (368a)

(b) LITANIES

Bb, 109 (74e)
Bb, 125
D, 195 (186d)
Eb, 243

(e) MISCELLANEOUS

God is our Refuge, 20
Scande coeli, 34
Veni Sancte Spiritus, 47
Benedictus sit, 117 (66a)
Te Deum, 141 (66b)
Ergo interest, 143 (73a)
Miserere, 85 (73s)

Cibavit eos, 44 (73u)
Quaerite primum, 86 (73v)
Regina coeli, 108 (74d)
Inter natos, 72 (74f)
De profundis, 93
Justum deduxit, 326 (93d)
Regina coeli, 127
Exsultate, jubilate, 165 (158a)
Sub tuum praesidium, 198 (158b)
Dixit et Magnificat, 193 (186g)
Misericordias Domini, 222 (205a)
Venite, populi, 260 (248a)
Alma Dei, 277 (272a)
Sancta Maria, 273
Regina coeli, 276 (321b)
O Gottes Lamm and Als aus Aegypten, 343(336c)
Ave verum corpus, 618

(f) CHURCH SONATAS

Eb, 67 (41h)	F, 244
Bb, 68 (41i)	D, 245
D, 69 (41k)	C, 263
D, 144 (124a)	G, 274 (271d)
F, 145 (124b)	C, 278 (271e)
Bb, 212	C, 328 (317c)
G, 241	C, 329 (317a)
F, 224 (241a)	C, 336 (336d)
A, 225 (241b)	

CANTATAS, etc.

Grabmusik, 42 (35a)
La Betulia liberata, 118 (74c)
Dir, Seele des Weltalls, 429 (420a)
Davidde penitente, 469
Die Maurerfreude, 471
Ein kleine deutsche Kantate, 619
Eine kleine Freimaurer-Kantate, 623

OPERAS

La finta semplice, 51 (46a)
Bastien und Bastienne, 50 (46b)
Mitridate, 87 (74a)
Lucio Silla, 135 (with ballet, 135a)
La finta giardiniera, 196
Il rè pastore, 208
Idomeneo, 366 (with ballet, 367)
Die Entführung aus dem Serail, 384
Der Schauspieldirektor, 486
Le nozze di Figaro, 492
Don Giovanni, 527
Così fan tutte, 588
Die Zauberflöte, 620
La clemenza di Tito, 621

MISCELLANEOUS AND INCOMPLETE STAGE WORKS

Die Schuldigkeit des ersten Gebotes (Part I), 35
Apollo et Hyacinthus, 38
Ascanio in Alba, 111
Il sogno di Scipione, 126
Thamos, König in Aegypten, 345 (336a)
Zaïde, 344 (336b)★
L'oca del Cairo, 422★
Lo sposo deluso, 430 (424a)★

ARIAS, etc.

(The opening words of the aria, or the preceding
recitative if there is one, are given.)

(a) FOR SOPRANO AND ORCHESTRA

Conservati fedele, 23
A Berenice, 70 (61c)
Per pietà, bell' idol mio, 78 (73b)
Fra cento affanni, 88 (73c)
O temerario Arbace, 79 (73d)
Misero me, 77 (73e)
Se ardire, 82 (73o)
Se tutti i mali, 83 (73p)
Non curo l'affetto, 74b
Voi avete un cor fedele, 217
Ah, lo previdi, 272
Alcandro, lo confesso, 294
Basta, vincesti, 486a (295a)
Popoli di Tessaglia, 316 (300b)
Kommet her ihr frechen, 146 (317b)
Ma che vi fece, 368
Misera, dove son, 369
A questo seno, 374
Der Liebe himmlisches Gefühl, 119 (382h)
Nehmet meinen Dank, 383
In te spero, 440 (383h)★
Mia speranza, 416
Vorrei spiegarvi, 418
No, no, che non sei, 419
Non più, tutto ascoltai, 490
Ch'io mi scordi, 505
Bella mia fiamma, 528
Ah se in ciel, 538
Al desio, di chi, 577
Alma grande, 578
Un moto di gioia, 579
Schon lacht, 580
Chi sà, chi sà, 582
Vado, ma dove, 583
Donne vaghe, 584a

(b) FOR ALTO AND ORCHESTRA

Ombra felice, 255

(c) FOR TENOR AND ORCHESTRA

Va, dal furor portata, 21 (19c)
Or che il dover, 36 (33i)
Ah, più tremar, 71★

Si mostra, 209
Con ossequio, 210
Clarice cara, 256
Se al labbro mio, 295
Müsst ich auch, 435 (416b)
Per pietà, non ricercate, 420
Misero, o sogno, 431 (425b)

(d) FOR BASS AND ORCHESTRA

Männer suchen, 433 (416c)
Così dunque tradisci, 432 (421a)
Alcandro, lo confesso, 512
Mentre ti lascio, 513
Ich möchte wohl der Kaiser, 539
Un bacio di mano, 541
Rivolgete a lui, 584
Per questa bella mano, 612
Io ti lascio, Anh.245 (621a)

DUETS, TRIOS, etc.

(a) WITH ACCOMPANIMENT FOR ORCHESTRA OR INSTRUMENTAL ENSEMBLE

Del gran regno, 434 (424b) (T, 2B)
Ecco quel fiero, 436 (2S, B)
Mi lagnerò tacendo, 437 (2S, B)
Se lontan, 438 (2S, B)★
Due pupille, 439 (2S, B)★
Luci care, 346 (439a) (2S, B)★
Dite almeno, 479 (S, T, 2B)
Mandina amabile, 480 (S, T, B)
Spiegarti non poss'io, 489 (S, T)
Grazie agl'inganni tuoi, 532 (S, T, B)
Più non si trovano, 549 (2S, B)
Caro mio, Anh.5 (571a) (S, 2T, B)

(b) WITH PIANO ACCOMPANIMENT

Welch ängstliches Beben, 389 (384) (2T)
Das Bandel, 441 (S, T, B)
Liebes Mädchen, 441c (2S or T, B)

LIEDER

An die Freude, 53 (43b)
Daphne, deine Rosenwagen, 52 (46c)
Die grossmütige Gelassenheit, 149 (125d)
Geheime Liebe, 150 (125e)
Die Zufriedenheit, 151 (125f)
Wie unglücklich, 147 (125g)
O heiliges Band, 148 (125h)
Ah, spiegarti, 178 (125i)
Ridente la calma, 152 (210a)
Oiseaux, si tous les ans, 307 (284d)
Dans un bois, 308 (295b)
Verdankt sei, 392 (430a)
An die Einsamkeit, 391 (340b)
An die Hoffnung, 390 (340c)

CANONS

(a) SONATAS

C, 279 (189d)
F, 280 (189e)
Bb, 281 (189f)
Eb, 282 (189g)
G, 283 (189h)
D, 284 (205b)
C, 309 (284b)
D, 311 (284c)
a, 310 (300d)
C, 330 (300h)

A, 331 (300i)
F, 332 (300k)
Bb, 333 (315c)
c, 457
Bb, 498a★†
C, 545
F, 533 & 494
F, Anh.135 & 138 (547a)
Bb, 570
D, 576

(b) VARIATIONS

A Dutch Song, 24
Willem von Nassau, 25
Mio caro Adone, 180 (173c)
Menuett von Fischer, 179 (189a)
Je suis Lindor, 354 (299a)
Ah, vous dirai-je, 265 (300e)
La belle Françoise, 353 (300f)
Lison dormait, 264 (315d)
March from Les Mariages samnites, 352 (374c)
Salve tu, Domine, 398 (416e)
Come un'agnello, 460 (454a)
Unser dummer Pöbel meint, 455
[An original theme], 500
Menuett von Duport, 573
Ein Weib ist, 613

(c) MISCELLANEOUS PIECES

Suite in C, 399 (385i)★
Fantasias: in c, 396 (385f); in d, 397 (385g); in c, 475
Fantasia and Fugue in C, 394 (383a)
Minuets: 1; 2; 4; 5; 94 (73h); 8 minuets, 315a (315g); 355 (594a)
Rondos: in D, 485; in a, 511
Allegros: in Bb, 3; in C, 9a (5a); in F, Anh.109b (15a); in g, 312 (189i); in Bb, 400 (372a)★; in Bb, Anh.136 (498a)
Andante in Bb, 9b (5b)
Andantino in Eb, 236 (588b)
Adagio in b, 540
Capriccio in C, 395 (300g)
Funeral March in c, 453a
Gigue in G, 574
43 further short pieces, 15a-15ss

(d) SONATAS FOR 4 HANDS

C, 19d
D, 381 (123a)
Bb, 358 (186c)
F, 497

G, 357 (497a)★
C, 521
D, 448 (375a) (for 2 pianos)

(e) MISCELLANEOUS PIECES FOR 4 HANDS

Fugue in g, 401 (375e)★
Variations in G, 501
Fugue in c, 426 (for 2 pianos)

(f) OTHER INSTRUMENTS

Adagio and Allegro in f for mechanical organ, 594
Fantasia in f for mechanical organ, 608
Andante in F for mechanical organ, 616
Adagio in C for harmonica, 356 (617a)

CHAMBER MUSIC

(a) KEYBOARD AND VIOLIN SONATAS

C, 6
D, 7
Bb, 8
G, 9
Bb, 10 ⎫
G, 11 ⎪
A, 12 ⎬ (with optional cello)
F, 13 ⎪
C, 14 ⎪
Bb, 15 ⎭
Eb, 26
G, 27
C, 28
D, 29
F, 30
Bb, 31
C, 46d ⎫ for violin and continuo
F, 46e ⎭
G, 301 (293a)
Eb, 302 (293b)

C, 303 (293c)
A, 305 (293d)
C, 296
e, 304 (300c)
D, 306 (300l)
Bb, 378 (317d)
G, 379 (373a)
F, 376 (374d)
F, 377 (374e)
Eb, 380 (374f)
C, 403 (385c)★
C, 404 (385d)★
A, 402 (385e)★
Bb, 454
Eb, 481
A, 526
F, 547
Allegro, Bb, 372★
Variations, 359 & 360 (374a & b)

(b) PIANO AND TWO OR MORE INSTRUMENTS

Trios: Bb, 254 (Divertimento)
       d, 442★
       G, 496
       Eb, 498 (with clarinet and viola)

Bb, 502
E, 542
C, 548
G, 564

Quartets: g, 478
          Eb, 493

Quintet: Eb, 452 (with oboe, clarinet, horn, bassoon)

(c) STRING QUARTETS

G, 80 (73f)
D, 155 (134a)
G, 156 (134b)
C, 157
F, 158
Bb, 159
Eb, 160 (159a)
F, 168
A, 169
C, 170
Eb, 171
Bb, 172

d, 173
G, 387
d, 421 (417b)
Eb, 428 (421b)
Bb, 458
A, 464
C, 465
D, 499
D, 575
Bb, 589
F, 590
Adagio and Fugue in c, 546

(d) STRING QUINTETS

Bb, 174
C, 515
g, 516

c, 406 (516b) (from Serenade, K.388)
D, 593
Eb, 614

(e) MISCELLANEOUS WORKS

String Duos: G, 423; Bb, 424
Duo for bassoon and cello: Bb, 292 (196c)
12 Duos for 2 horns, 487 (496a)
String Trios: Bb, 266 (271f); 404a (4 preludes to fugues by J. S. and W. F. Bach);
  Eb, 563
Flute Quartets: G, 285; G, 285a; C, Anh.171 (285b)†; A, 298
Oboe Quartet: F, 370 (368b)
Horn Quintet: Eb, 407 (386c)
Clarinet Quintet: A, 581
Adagio and Allegro in c for harmonica, flute, oboe, violin and cello, 617

SYMPHONIES

1 in Eb, 16
4 in D, 19
5 in Bb, 22
– in F, 76 (42a)
6 in F, 43
7 in D, 45
– in G, Anh.221 (45a)
– in Bb, Anh.214 (45b)
8 in D, 48
– in D, 81 (73l)
– in D, 97 (73m)
– in D, 95 (73n)
11 in D, 84 (73q)
10 in G, 74
– in Bb, Anh.216 (74g)
– in F, 75
9 in C, 73 (75a)
12 in G, 110 (75b)
– in C, 96 (111b)
13 in F, 112
14 in A, 114
15 in G, 124
16 in C, 128
17 in G, 129

18 in F, 130
19 in Eb, 132
20 in D, 133
21 in A, 134
22 in C, 162
27 in G, 199 (162a)
23 in D, 181 (162b)
26 in Eb, 184 (166a)
24 in Bb, 182 (166c)
28 in C, 200 (173e)
25 in g, 183
29 in A, 201 (186a)
30 in D, 202 (186b)
31 in D, 297 (300a) (Paris)
32 in G, 318
33 in Bb, 319
34 in C, 334
35 in D, 385 (Haffner)
36 in C, 425 (Linz)
38 in D, 504 (Prague)
39 in Eb, 543
40 in g, 550
41 in C, 551 (Jupiter)

DIVERTIMENTOS, SERENADES, etc.

(a) FOR WIND INSTRUMENTS

2 each of oboes, horns, bassoons:
F, 213
Bb, 240
Eb, 252 (240a)
F, 253
Bb, 270
Eb, 289 (271g)†

2 each of oboes, clarinets, horns, bassoons:
Eb, Anh.226 (196e)†
Bb, Anh.227 (196f)†
Eb, 375 (originally without oboes)
c, 388 (384a)

2 each of oboes, cors anglais, clarinets, horns, bassoons:
Bb, 186 (159b)
Eb, 166 (159d)

2 each of oboes, clarinets, basset-horns, bassoons, 4 horns, double-bass:
Bb, 361 (370a)

3 basset-horns
5 divertimentos in Bb, Anh.229 (439b) (No. 5†)

2 flutes, 5 trumpets, 4 drums:
C, 187 (159c)
C, 188 (240b)

Miscellaneous movements:
Adagio for 2 clarinets and 3 basset-horns, 411 (440a)
Adagio for 2 basset-horns and bassoon, 410 (440d)
Adagio for clarinet and 3 basset-horns, Anh. 94 (580a)★

(b) WITH STRINGS
(certain of the serenades etc. have particular marches associated with them; in these
cases the numbers of the marches are added in square brackets)
Galimathias Musicum, 32
Serenade in D, 100 (62a)
Divertimento in G, 63
Cassation in Bb, 99 (63a)
Divertimento in Eb, 113
Divertimento in D, 131
Divertimento in D, 136 (125a)
Divertimento in F, 137 (125b)
Divertimento in Bb, 138 (125c)
Finalmusik in D, 185 (167a) [189 (167b)]
Divertimento in D, 205 (173a) [290 (173b)]
Serenade in D, 203 (189b) [237 (189c)]
Serenade in D, 204 (213a) [215 (213b)]
Serenata Notturna in D, 239
Divertimento in F, 247 [248]
Serenade in D, 250 (248b) (Haffner) [249]
Divertimento in D, 251
Notturno in D, 286 (269a)
Divertimento in Bb, 287 (271b)
Serenade in D, 320 (Posthorn) [2 marches, 335 (320a)]
Divertimento in D, 334 (320b) [445 (320c)]
Musical Joke in F, 522
Eine Kleine Nachtmusik in G, 525

MISCELLANEOUS ORCHESTRAL MUSIC

March in C, 214
2 Marches in C and D, 408 (383e and 385a)
Symphony finales: in D, 120 (111a); in D, 163 (141a); in D, 121 (207a); in C, 102 (213c)
Symphony minuet: in C, 409 (383f)
Symphony introduction: in G, 444 (425a) (Symphony No. 37)
Masonic Funeral Music, 477 (479a)
Ballet, Les petits riens, Anh. 10 (299b)

DANCES

(The number in each set is shown in bold)

(a) MINUETS

7, 65a (61a)	**16,** 176
19, 103 (61d)	**3,** 363
6, 104 (61e)	**5,** 461 (448a)
6, 105 (61f)	**2** (with contredanses), 463 (448c)
2, 61g	**12,** 568
6, 61h	**12,** 585
1, 64	**6,** 599
1, 122 (73t)	**4,** 601
6, 164 (130a)	**2,** 604

(b) GERMAN DANCES AND LÄNDLER

6, 509	**6,** 600
6, 536	**4,** 602
6, 567	**3,** 605
6, 571	**6,** 606
12, 586	**1,** 611

(c) CONTREDANSES

1, 123 (73g)	**2,** 565
3, 101 (250a)	**1,** 587
4, 267 (271c)	**3** & overture, 106 (588a)
6, 462 (448b)	**2,** 603
1, 534	**1,** 607
1, 535	**5,** 609
3, 535a	**1,** 610

CONCERTOS

(a) VIOLIN

Bb, 207
D, 211
G, 216
D, 218
A, 219
D, 271a (271i)†
Eb, 268 (365b)†
Adagio in E, 261 [for 219]
Rondo in Bb, 269 (261) [for 207]
Rondo in C, 373
Concertone in C, 190 (166b) (2 violins)
Sinfonia Concertante in Eb, 364 (320d) (violin and viola)

(b) WIND INSTRUMENTS

Bassoon, Bb, 191 (186e)
Flute, G, 313 (285c)
Oboe or Flute, C or D, 314 (285d)
Andante for Flute, C, 315 (285e) [for 313]
Sinfonia Concertante, oboe, clarinet, horn, bassoon, Eb, Anh. 9 (297b)†
Flute and Harp, C, 299 (297c)
Rondo for Horn, Eb, 371*
Horn, D, 412 (386b)
Horn, Eb, 417
Horn, Eb, 447
Horn, Eb, 495
Clarinet, A, 622

(c) PIANO

D, 175	d, 466
Bb, 238	C, 467
C, 246	Eb, 482
Eb, 271	A, 488
A, 414 (386a)	c, 491
F, 413 (387a)	C, 503
C, 415 (387b)	D, 537 (Coronation)
Eb, 449	Bb, 595
Bb, 450	Rondo in D, 382
D, 451	Rondo in A, 386
G, 453	F, 242 (3 pianos)
Bb, 456	Eb, 365 (316a) (2 pianos)
F, 459	Cadenzas, 624 (626a)

ARRANGEMENTS

Orchestrations of works by Handel: Acis and Galatea, 566; Messiah, 572; Alexander's Feast, 591; Ode for St. Cecilia's Day, 592

Orchestration of a duet (? by Schack), Nun liebes Weibchen, 625 (592a)

Piano Concertos: 3, after sonatas by J. C. Bach, 107 (21b); 4, after sonatas by Schobert, Raupach, Honauer, Eckardt, C. P. E. Bach etc., 37, 39, 40, 41

Fugues for strings, transcribed from J. S. and W. F. Bach, 404a and 405

Dating Table

The following table can be used for ascertaining the probable date of any work from its Köchel (3rd edn.) number. Since the dates of completion of most of Mozart's works are uncertain, it cannot be used as an exact guide. Opposite each year is given the number of the year's probable first completed work.

1762	**K.1**		1777	**K.270**
1763	**K.5a**		1778	**K.285a**
1764	**K.9**		1779	**K.315g**
1765	**K.19**		1780	**K.336d**
1766	**K.24**		1781	**K.366**
1767	**K.34**		1782	**K.382**
1768	**K.45**		1783	**K.416**
1769	**K.61a**		1784	**K.448a**
1770	**K.73a**		1785	**K.464**
1771	**K.74b**		1786	**K.485**
1772	**K.114a**		1787	**K.509**
1773	**K.157**		1788	**K.533**
1774	**K.186a**		1789	**K.569**
1775	**K.196**		1790	**K.588**
1776	**K.238**		1791	**K.595**

Select Bibliography

Abert, H., *Wolfgang Amadeus Mozart*, 2 vols, Leipzig, 1923–4
Anderson, Emily, *The Letters of Mozart and His Family*, 2 vols, New York, St Martin's Press, 1966; London, Macmillan, 1966
Bauer, W. A. and Deutsch, O. E., *Mozart: Briefe und Aufzeichnungen*, 4 vols, Kassel, Bärenreiter, 1962–3
Blom, E., *Mozart*, New York, Farrar, Straus & Giroux, 1949; London, Dent, 1962
Dent, E. J., *Mozart's Operas*, London, Oxford University Press, 1947; New York, Oxford University Press, 1960
Deutsch, O. E., *Mozart: A Documentary Biography*, Stanford, California, Stanford University Press, 1965; London, Black, 1965
—— *Mozart: Memoirs by His Friends*, New York, Hillary House, 1958
Einstein, A., *Mozart: His Character, His Work*, New York, Oxford University Press, 1945; London, Cassell, 1956
Hutchings, A. J. B., *A Companion to Mozart's Piano Concertos*, London, Oxford University Press, 1950; New York, Oxford University Press, 1957
Köchel, L. von, *Chronologisch-thematisches Verzeichnis sämtlicher Tonwerke Wolfgang Amade Mozarts*, 7th edn, Wiesbaden, Breitkopf & Härtel, 1967
Landon, H. C. Robbins and Mitchell, D. (ed.), *The Mozart Companion*, New York, Oxford University Press, 1956; London, Faber, 1965
Lang, P. H., *The Creative World of Mozart*, New York, W. W. Norton, 1963
Schenk, E., *Mozart and His Times*, New York, Alfred A. Knopf, 1959; London, Secker & Warburg, 1960
Schneider, O. and Algatzy, A., *Mozart-Handbuch*, Vienna, Hollinek, 1962
Wyzewa, T. de and Saint-Foix, G. de, *W. A. Mozart, sa Vie Musicale et son Oeuvre*, 5 vols, the last 3 by Saint-Foix alòne, Bruges, Desclée de Brouwer, 1912–46

Mozart's keepsake

Index of Works

References to works in the chronological discussion under forms are not included in this index; page references to the discussion of each group are given alongside headings. Works are given in the same order as in the list of works, pp. 171-181. References to musical examples, illustrations from manuscripts and scenes from operas are given in bold.

Index of People and Places

A

Aachen, 10
Abel, C. F., 80, **122**, 123, 124
Accademia Filarmonica: *see* Bologna
Acis and Galatea: see Handel, G. F.
Adamberger, V., **53**
Adlgasser, C., 19, 77
Agujari, L., 27
Alceste: see Gluck, C. W. von
Allegri, G., *Miserere*, 23
Ambrogetti, G., **155**
Amsterdam, 16
Anderson, E., 12n
André, J., 71
Anfossi, P., 81, 83, 99
– *La finta giardiniera*, 83
– *La vera costanza*, **83**
– *Il curioso indiscreto*, 99
Antwerp, 14, 16
Arco, Count, 47
Ariadne: see Benda, G.
Armida: see Salieri, A.
Attwood, T., 59
Augsburg, 7, 9, 17, 33
Austria, Archduchess Josepha of, 19
Austria, Emperor Joseph II of, 8, 20-21, 54, 69, 84
Austria, Emperor Leopold II of, 69, 70, 73, 74, 75
Austria, Empress Maria Theresa of, 8, 27, 28, 46, 162

B

Bach, C. P. E., 77, 90, 102
– *Essay on the True Art of Keyboard Playing*, 77
Bach, J. C., 12, 38, **79**, 80, 81, 83, 91, 123, 125, 126, 131, 135, 137f
– Symphony in G minor, Op. 6 No. 6, 81
– Piano Concerto in G, Op. 1 No. 6, **80**
– *Zanaïda*, 14
Bach, J. S., 12, 53, 68, 86, 87, 88, 101, 115, 135, 163
– *Singet dem Herrn*, 68
Bachmann, S., 17
Baden, 69, 71
Barbier de Séville, Le: see Beaumarchais, P. C. de, *and* Paisiello, G.
Barone de Torreforte, Il: see Piccini, N.
Barrington, D., 14
Bavaria, Elector Maximilian of, 8, 9, 29, 32, 40
Bavaria, Elector Carl Theodor of, 40, 45, 96; *see also* Palatinate, Elector of
Bavaria, Electress (wife of above), 42; *see also* Palatinate, Electress of
Beaumarchais, P. C. de, 60, **62**, 153
– *Le Barbier de Séville*, 60
– *Le Mariage de Figaro*, 60
Beecke, I. von, 34, **40**
Beethoven, L. van, 65, 87, 101, 102, 103, 110, 123, 133, 158, 160, 163

Acknowledgements: The author is grateful to his wife for criticising and typing the manuscript; to Charles Cudworth and Michael Whewell for criticising it; and to Angela McNelly for preparing the index.

Iconography

A. Armstrong-Jones, 48-9

R. Betz, Munich, 146, 147

Bibliothèque Nationale, Paris, 36, 127

British Museum (by kind permission of the Trustees), 6, 12, 14, 20, 23, 29, 38, 39, 47, 50, 58, 59, 61, 64, 67, 74, 76, 82, 85, 89, 91, 98, 106, 109, 111, 120, 122, 129, 138, 142, 150, 154, 161, 166; R.C.M. Collection, 141; Stefan Zweig Collection, 33, 54, 63, 105, 116, 131

G. Gravett, Hurstpierpoint, 60

Hirsch, Nördlingen, 119 (original in Schloss Wallerstein)

Historisches Museum der Stadt Frankfurt, 70

Hunterian Museum, Glasgow, 57

E. N. Kitson, London, 13, 18, 66, 114, 152

L. P. Morley, 24 (original in Pendlebury Library, Cambridge)

Libraire Hachette, Paris, 62

Opera Magazine, 69, 155, 156, 159

Philips Records, 9, 92

Radio Times Hulton Picture Library, 79

Harold Rosenthal Collection, 149, 157

Salzburg, Mozarteum (by kind permission), 2, 11, 15, 17, 25, 26, 35, 44, 87, 100, 102, 132 134, 144, 184

Salzburg, Museum Carolino Augusteum, 21, 30, 95

Silhouettes by E. N. Kitson, after 18th-century originals, 40, 41, 43, 51, 53, 72, 151, 162